A Pictorial History of
the United States Customs Service

A Pictorial History
of the United States
Customs Service

From Colonial Times to the Present Day

by ARTHUR SETTEL

With a Preface by U.S. Commissioner of Customs Vernon D. Acree

CROWN PUBLISHERS, INC., NEW YORK

Printed in the United States of America
Published simultaneously in Canada by General Publishing Company Limited

Library of Congress Cataloging in Publication Data

Settel, Arthur.
    A pictorial history of the United States Customs Service.

    Includes index.
    1. United States. Bureau of Customs—History—Pictorial works. I. Title.
HJ6622.A6 · 1975   353.008′27   75-28211
ISBN 0-517-51907-0

Dedicated to the men and women of the U.S.
Customs Service who, by their devotion and dedication to
the ideals of good government, have set an example to all
other civil servants and made this arm of the Treasury Department
an honored symbol of competence, skill, and integrity.

Acknowledgments

The author wishes to acknowledge his debt of gratitude to many individuals, without whose contributions, suggestions, and helpfulness this book would not have been possible. Among them are the following: Court of Claims Judge and former Commissioner of Customs Philip Nichols, Jr.; former U.S. Commissioners of Customs Lester D. Johnson and Myles J. Ambrose; Edwin F. Rains, former Deputy Commissioner; Dorothy Ladue, Mary Stim, Christine Frazer Ligoske, William Steo, Barry McCahill, Merced Perez-Trevino, and Mark McCormack, all of the Customs Service. A special vote of thanks goes to Ernest Chambre, archivist and historian, of New York, who long encouraged the development of this book.

Many of the more recent photographs in this book were taken by Harold Wise, producer, cameraman, and photographer par excellence, presently chief of the Audio-Visual Presentations Branch of the Public Information Division of the Customs Service.

Last but not least, I am indebted to my wife, Helen R. Settel, who devoted many days and weeks at the typewriter, as well as reading copy for this book, and to others too numerous to mention who willingly helped with information and background material on Customs matters.

Contents

Preface

By the second act of the First Congress, our Founding Fathers recognized the importance of a system of tariffs to raise revenue for the new republic. So important to our country's survival were customs duties considered that the press of that time hailed the July 4, 1789, Tariff Act as "the second Declaration of Independence." And so important to President George Washington was the new Customs Service, created four weeks later, that he appointed his most trusted confidants—former Revolutionary War officers and signers of the Declaration of Independence—to posts as collectors of customs.

This, then, is the story of the Customs Service. Born of a desperate need for funds by a struggling infant government, it evolved into more than just a revenue-producing agency. As the only federal agency in most of the nation's ports, and along our land and sea borders, Customs soon became responsible for paying pensions, collecting seamen's dues, overseeing the infant Coast Guard, and enforcing a myriad of other federal laws. By the 1970s these statutes numbered more than four hundred; and two hundred of these Customs now applies on behalf of some forty other federal agencies.

During his twelve years as public information officer for the Customs Service, Arthur Settel collected anecdotes, photographs, documents, and memorabilia of the service. He was fascinated by the colorful history of the agency and longed to write a book about Customs. This manuscript was completed after his retirement in June 1974 and sent to the publisher just before his death in April 1975.

Mr. Settel's book links the colorful past with the intriguing present. Along with Customs officers Nathaniel Hawthorne and Herman Melville, the reader meets Wanda, the drug-detecting Labrador retriever, and TECS, a computer—two of the tools that reflect the wide-ranging contemporary activities and technological capabilities of the U.S. Customs Service.

This book is not just a collection of pictures of the men, women, and events which shaped the second oldest federal agency in the government. In many ways it is a history of the United States, itself, for no other federal agency has had a greater impact on our nation's growth or has been more intimately involved in the momentous events which shaped our nation. From the Embargo Act of 1807 and the War of 1812, through the decades of expansion and the great Civil War; from the rum-running days of Prohibition to the national emergencies of two world wars; from the air piracy crisis of the early 1970s to the unending war against narcotics smuggling, Customs has been involved. Throughout our country's history, Customs officers were there—frequently on the front lines, and always quietly in the background, collecting and protecting the revenue that financed the nation from 1789 until the twentieth century.

Mr. Settel intended his book to be a monument to the persons and events which have made the Customs Service a respected institution. In so doing, he left another monument—a memorial to one man's faith in the institutions of government.

VERNON D. ACREE

Commissioner of Customs

A Pictorial History of
the United States Customs Service

A dramatic moment for Customs agents, the
arrest of two smugglers and the seizure of
their narcotics-laden van.

chapter one

The Customs Story: A Profile

The Customs story is in large part the story of the American dream. The United States Customs Service gave first expression to the sovereignty of the infant republic, destined to survive and prosper over enormous obstacles until it achieved world preeminence in virtually every field of human endeavor.

The steps marking America's growth and expansion from a group of quarreling, jealous states to a closely knit, united entity were paced by the development of the Customs Service, which antedated the creation of what is now its parent department, the United States Treasury Department, by one whole month. Thus the child is older than the parent.

The footprints of U.S. Customs are indelibly imprinted on the sands of time. They mark out the story of our country. When in 1794 it became necessary for the new nation to create a navy for defense and survival, Customs revenues provided the funds to construct the *Constitution* (sometimes known as Old Ironsides), the *United States*, and the *Constellation*. When the Barbary wars broke out in 1801 and Americans were held for ransom in Algeria, the one million dollars the United States had to pay for their freedom came from Customs receipts. Customs duties paid for the planning and building of the capital city of Washington, the United States Military Academy at West Point, and the Naval Academy at Annapolis. Customs revenues provided the funds for the Louisiana Purchase in 1803, and all or part of thirteen new states were eventually carved from this former French territory, doubling the area of the country. Customs revenues made possible the purchase of Florida and Oregon and of large areas of territory above the Rio Grande from Mexico. When in 1835 the national debt was reduced to zero—perhaps for the first and last time in American history—Customs made it possible.

When narcotics became a national epidemic, it was the Customs Service that was designated the nation's "first line of defense" against the smuggled drugs that engulfed the country. When the hijacking of aircraft became a threat to the welfare of the traveling public, Customs was called upon to provide sky marshals to restore safety in the skies.

In peace and in war, through crises and periods of tranquillity, the Customs Service has remained a rock of Gibraltar. Its agents have guarded our borders and ports of entry against all kinds of contraband, ranging from destructive plant life to lethal narcotic drugs. Its trained specialists have protected the Treasury of the

Examining imported watch mechanisms to determine the number of jeweled movements and other features that will affect the rate of duty to be applied.

United States against fraud. Its chemists have prevented toxic substances from entering the nation's commerce, threatening the lives of unsuspecting citizens. Its fiscal experts have ensured that the revenues collected are correct and legal and go where they are intended—into the federal government's central treasury. Its staff of commodity import specialists has kept falsely identified goods from being introduced into the economy. Its patrols have interdicted smuggled gold, diamonds, watch movements, undervalued items, products of cheap foreign labor illegally imported, marihuana, hashish, heroin, and cocaine.

The Customs Service has a mystique; it has always been much more than a faceless government agency. Its staff can lay claim to the lowest turnover rate of any branch of government—a sure sign of esprit de corps and high morale. Thirty-, thirty-five-, and forty-year service pins are routine. Fifty-year veterans are not uncommon. The traditions of the service are passed down from one gen-

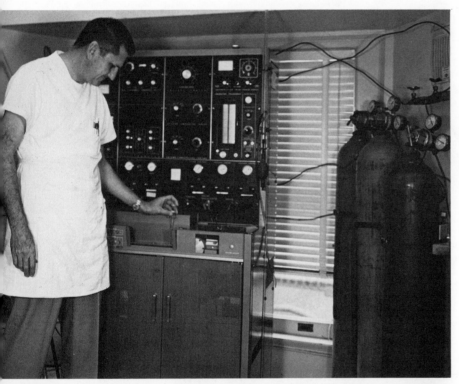

Chemistry has always been an important tool of Customs. This gas chromatography equipment can detect extremely small quantities of narcotics.

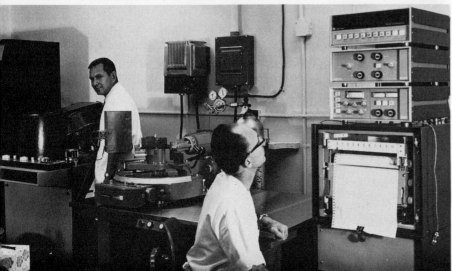

Here Customs chemists use X-ray diffraction-fluorescence techniques to analyze the composition of inorganic metals and alloys.

eration to the next. Every clerk-typist and messenger knows that Herman Melville, Nathaniel Hawthorne, and Chester A. Arthur were at one time Customs employees.

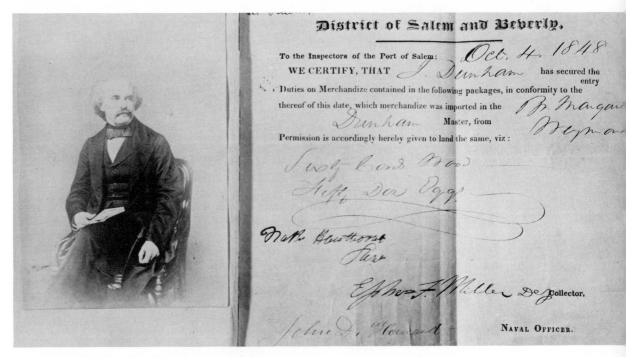

A picture of Nathaniel Hawthorne and an 1848 Customs document bearing his signature. Hawthorne worked as a surveyor of Customs at Salem.

A tightly knit organization with its own code of honor, the Customs Service is dispersed over a far-flung geographical area, spanning continents and oceans, and 185 years of history. It has no official coat of arms, although the shoulder patch of the Customs inspector serves the same purpose and appears on citations and official documents. Inspectors, Customs patrol officers, and warehouse officers wear uniforms, but the service is a source of pride for all employees, in and out of uniform.

Loyalty to the long and honored tradition of the U.S. Customs Service is more binding than any insignia or vow of obedience could make it. This loyalty reveals itself in a very low rate of personnel dereliction. In those circumstances where corruption is discovered, Customs is ready and willing to investigate, prefer charges, and bring to trial those of its own people who have broken the faith.

The U.S. Customs Service has a thousand faces. To the average traveler return-

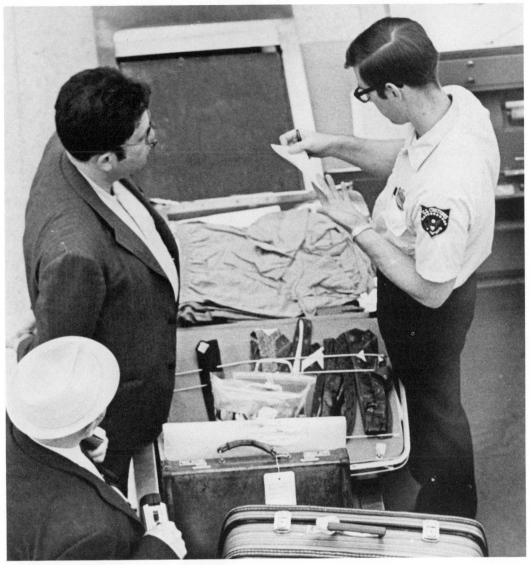

This is the kind of Customs inspection that has become so familiar and routine to many Americans in the age of air travel, and for most it is their only contact with the U.S. Customs Service.

Though travel by ocean liner has declined, it has by no means disappeared. Here a Customs inspector examines luggage belonging to returning travellers at Holland America's Pier 40 in New York.
Courtesy The Port of New York Authority.

ing from a trip overseas, Customs is the man in a blue uniform who searches luggage, shakes socks, fingers the bottom of suitcases, and asks: "Do you have anything to declare?" To the importer of foreign manufactures, Customs is the man who appraises and classifies the merchandise and then collects duties on it. To the smuggler of narcotics, Customs is an oversized watchdog who blocks his way when he is about to make a big bundle of cash in this, the world's most lucrative market for illicit drugs. To the ship's crew, Customs is the man in fatigue outfit, flashlight in hand, who with his teammates goes through the ship's locker rooms, hold, offices, and heads, searching for illegal imports.

To the business executive engaged in international trade, Customs is the quiet man in pin-striped suit who goes through the firm's books with a magnifying glass searching for undervalued merchandise or undeclared imports. To the travel agent, Customs is a necessary adjunct to successful tourist travel —bothersome but unavoidable. To the aged and infirm who return from a trip abroad, Customs is the good samaritan who helps with the luggage, pushes the wheelchair, and expedites them through the maze of red tape and clearances all travelers must go through. To the budget and fiscal analysts in the Treasury Department, Customs is a prime producer of revenue—to the tune of $4.5 billions annually, no small sum when computed against the Customs Service's budget of $250 million. To the importer of pornography, Customs is "big brother," exercising censorship over prurient film sequences or obscene books and magazines.

The Customs Service is people. It is the plainclothes investigator, staking out a suspect in the dark alleys of the New Orleans waterfront. It is the amiable ambassador of goodwill who welcomes you back after a trip abroad, or who hopes you enjoy your stay in the United States. It is the attractive young interpreter who helps the non-English-speaking foreigner find his way out of the airport to locate waiting relatives. It is an import specialist, seated behind a desk at a customhouse, examining manifests and other shipping documents, preparatory to the payment of Customs duties. It is the suntanned pilot of a Customs aircraft doing dawn patrol duty along the Gulf Coast. It is the patient and skilled dog handler, gently coaxing his German shepherd as the animal sniffs his way through a mountain of packages in a U.S. post office mail room, searching for narcotics. It is the staff officer, clambering aboard a transoceanic ship arriving at quarantine in New York harbor, to check the Customs declarations of passenger arrivals. It is the attorney at a federal courthouse, arguing for the people of the United States in a potential fraud case. It is the undercover agent, penetrating a drug smuggling conspiracy, risking life and limb in an effort to trap the criminals.

Customs is all of these people and many more—clerks and typists, messengers and mail examiners, chemists and mechanics, financial analysts and managers, pilots of boats and drivers of souped-up motor vehicles, patrol officers on horseback (yes, even as recently as 1975) along the Mexican border, and port directors who carry out a myriad of duties for their own and other government agencies.

Customs personnel are stationed at hundreds of ports of entry, stretching out like a string of beads along the main coasts, the Canadian and Mexican borders, the remote parts of Alaska in the frozen north, and the blistering southland of

Much of the work of Customs takes place behind the scenes and is unknown to the general public. Here Customs appraisers at a New York pier examine imported merchandise and compare the actual items to their description on the manifest.

Here parcels mailed from foreign countries are distributed to import specialists for examination. After the articles in the parcels are classified and the duty on them is determined, they are given to other Customs officers for repacking and delivery to the post office. The postman collects the duty for Customs.

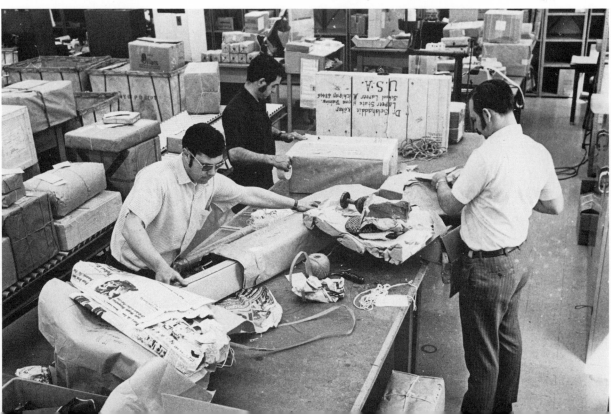

Texas and Arizona. They are found at ports in Hawaii, Puerto Rico, and the Virgin Islands, and at inland ports like Butte, Montana; Bismarck, North Dakota; and Pittsburgh, Pennsylvania. They guard some 96,000 miles of border with a force of less than 15,000—half the strength of the Customs Service in the Federal Republic of Germany. In recent times more than 260 million persons went through U.S. Customs in a single calendar year—more than the entire population of the United States. Customs handles $100 billions in imports each year—more than the imports of the rest of the western hemisphere and Europe combined. Customs carries out and enforces more than 400 laws and statutes, 200 of them for forty other U.S. government agencies, in addition to enforcing the incredibly complex tariff laws of the United States.

It would be difficult to identify those aspects of life in America that are not affected by the operations, plans, and policies of Customs. From the moment you get out of bed in the morning until you retire at night, your life must in some manner be touched by some activity of this agency, no matter how obscure or seemingly remote.

Whether you are dining out on imported chinaware or attending a foreign-made film; making snapshots with a Japanese or German camera; operating a motor vehicle produced in whole or in part by workers in another country; reading a newspaper printed on Canadian or Swedish newsprint; purchasing an electrical appliance that has been assembled in a Mexican factory; whatever your profession or station in life—whatever your interests, hobbies or pursuits—U.S. Customs has had some influence upon the quality or price or availability of the products you use.

The phenomenal growth of the country has made it inevitable that additional burdens would be placed upon the men and women of Customs. When the service first came into being, sailboats and horse-drawn vehicles were the principal

Customs chemists in a New Orleans laboratory. Many imports require chemical analysis to determine if they contain narcotics, harmful ingredients, or substances that require special tariff valuation.

A somewhat unusual seizure for Customs, a collection of German military trophies and uniforms from the two world wars.

A collection of miscellaneous contraband seized in Philadelphia, including rings, jewelry, watches, cameras and film, and diamonds in envelopes. Items such as these are not illegal per se, but when they are not declared and duty is not paid, Customs may confiscate them.

This shipment of two thousand Canadian coins, many of them special commemorative twenty-dollar gold pieces, was taken from two smugglers as they crossed the border into Montana.
Courtesy of the *Great Falls Leader*.

This shipment of undeclared liquor arrived aboard ship, concealed in various places, including lifeboats, bulkheads, and the engine room.

means of conveyance. The steamboat was followed by the railroad. Then automobiles became a significant factor, and today travel by air has assumed first place in global transportation.

The use of aircraft in international traffic is relentlessly expanding and countless new airports of entry have been designated to take care of the travel explosion. With improvements in aircraft and their increased use in the transportation of passengers and cargo in jumbo jets, the monitoring of air transportation becomes increasingly critical to Customs. Aircraft are required to land at designated airports of entry or suffer the imposition of a penalty. Likewise, automobiles and other vehicles must report at regular Customs ports of entry upon their arrival from Canada or Mexico.

The increase in tourist travel by air, cars, and vessels has severely taxed the facilities of the service, not only in connection with the regular entry and examination of baggage and personal effects, but also in the detection of the smuggling of contraband.

Mobile radio communications are available and in use wherever needed, while highly trained detector dogs provide a specialized interdiction capability. Customs boats and sensor-equipped aircraft and helicopters lend more muscle to enforcement operations. Highly visible, mobile tactical units operate around the clock, further strengthening the protective screen against the organized traffickers who make their living by smuggling.

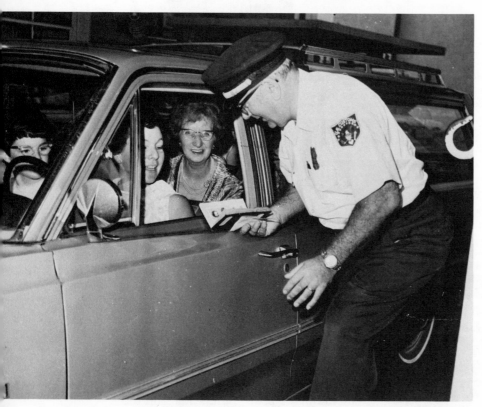

In the twentieth century the automobile has revolutionized Customs inspection procedures as much as the airplane. Here a Customs inspector examines the passports of Canadian tourists crossing from Windsor, Ontario, to Detroit.
Courtesy *The Detroit News*.

CUSTOMS DECLARATION	AIRCRAFT NO. AND TYPE	OPERATED BY	ARRIVAL AIRPORT	DATE OF ARRIVAL	PIECES OF BAGGAGE
(See Instructions on Reverse)	C141-40653	MAC	Ellington AFB, Tex	11 Feb 71	None

LAST NAME, FIRST, MIDDLE INITIAL

Shepard, Alan B.

ADDRESS IN THE UNITED STATES

I DEPARTED THE UNITED STATES ON _____

(If 3 days or less, state hour) _____

DATE LAST EXEMPTION UPON ENTERING THE UNITED STATES FROM A FOREIGN COUNTRY

PERSONS ON THIS DECLARATION *(Check applicable box)*
- [✓] MILITARY
- [ ] MILITARY DEPENDENTS
- [ ] CIVILIAN
- [✓] PASSENGER
- [ ] CREW MEMBER

NO. OF PERSONS ON THIS DECLARATION

STATUS FOR RETURN *(Check applicable box)*
- [ ] LEAVE
- [ ] PERMANENT CHANGE OF STATION
- [✓] TERMINATION OF TEMPORARY DUTY

DESCRIPTION	VALUE OR COST	TARIFF DESCRIPTION	RATE	DUTY	TAX
None					
		Passed Free Without			
		Entry, Section 321, T.A. 130			
		J.R.H.			
TOTAL DECLARED VALUE		**TOTAL**		$	$

I declare all items listed above were acquired by me in foreign countries, which list is correct to the best of my knowledge and belief. I further declare that all articles are for my personal use or intended as gifts for others, except as noted.

Alan B. Shepard
SIGNATURE OF DECLARANT

CASHIER'S STAMP

TOTAL COLLECTED
$

INTERNAL REVENUE TAX
SPIRITS	$_____
WINE	$_____
BEER	$_____
DUTY	$_____

DATE
11 Feb 71

CUSTOMS INSPECTOR SIGNATURE

AF FORM 653 NOV 66

PREVIOUS EDITION WILL BE USED

A sign of the times: the Customs declaration of astronaut Alan B. Shepard, filed upon his return to the United States from outer space on February 11, 1971.

The Customs Service's inspection activities are an integral part of its other enforcement efforts. Modern computer technology and communications have accelerated the processing of the unending stream of travelers and vehicles of all types crossing the borders. These same modern aids are used by import specialists in processing commercial cargo shipments, enabling them to be more selective in how and to what degree shipments must be examined. Complementing these multifaceted activities are the efforts of the special agents, the agency's professional investigators.

Although the Customs Service's antismuggling activities may appear to be the most dramatic and colorful part of its work, the more prosaic operations of entry, examination, and appraisal of merchandise remain the backbone of the service. When one considers that hundreds of thousands of articles are imported every day, ranging from common pins to large intricate machines; from cheap trinkets and toys to expensive jewelry and involved scientific apparatus; in fact, practically every known article of commerce in use today, it becomes apparent that Customs specialists must possess a thorough and detailed knowledge of the Tariff Act, of the Customs regulations that are based on the Act, as well as countless other laws and regulations affecting the importation of everyday necessities and luxuries.

Recently, a Customs official, in a major policy speech, quipped that our great national sport was not baseball or football, but the widespread and never-ending game of trying to "rip off the government." Of course, this jest was nothing more than that. But the painful truth is that if the federal government were able to collect all of the revenue that is due, it could probably pay off the national debt. Does this mean that most of our citizens are cheating, trying to get away with whatever is possible without getting caught? The facts do not support this sweeping generalization. But, on the other hand, defrauding the treasury is so common and widespread that the American taxpayers are spending millions of dollars—through the U.S. Customs Service and other agencies—to detect and stop it.

Fraud, the deliberate attempt to evade payment of import duties by falsifying the country of origin, or by misrepresenting the current market value of an import in its country of origin, or by tampering with the books of a corporation to conceal the true cost of foreign labor, has become one of the major preoccupations of Customs investigators. In recent years, not a day goes by without charges of fraud being preferred against major corporations, some of them household names. The agent-investigators, many of them former certified public accountants, move swiftly on receipt of a "hot tip" from an informer. They dig into the records of multimillion-dollar corporate structures and their subsidiaries and frequently come up with almost unbelievable evidence of fraud, sometimes due to ignorance of the law, sometimes deliberate. The penalties are heavy, sometimes running into millions of dollars for a single violation. During the stewardship of Vernon D. Acree, the present Commissioner, the Customs Service zeroed in on hundreds of corporations, their number limited only by the availability of agents possessing the skills to perform these unique duties, which call for a high degree of financial expertise.

Inspection of arriving vessels at major
seaports is also a responsibility of Customs.
In these pictures Customs inspectors are
seen examining the cargo of freighters and
tankers, checking a ship's manifest, and
probing into some of the more remote areas
belowdecks where contraband articles
might be hidden.

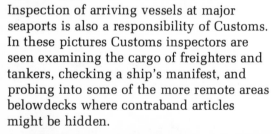

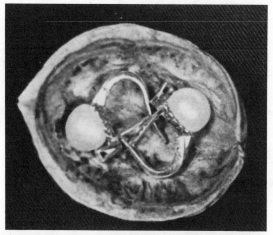

Narcotics aren't the only things smuggled into the country. Individuals as well as organized groups are continually trying to avoid paying duties on a whole range of objects covered by the tariff laws. Understating the value of particular imports is one very common technique, but very often the objects are concealed and not declared at all. Here an attempt was made to smuggle pearl earrings inside walnut shells.

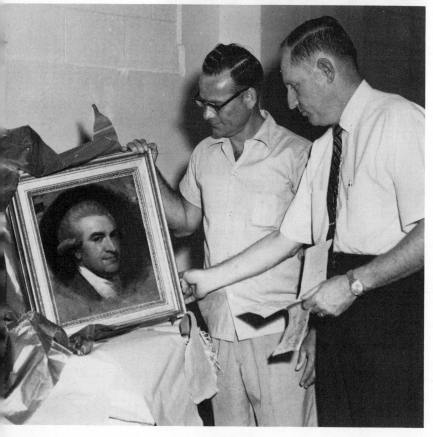

Customs import specialists remove an expensive oil painting from its shipping crate. The skyrocketing prices of art objects and the growing tendency to use art as a form of investment have forced Customs inspectors to become expert art appraisers in order to prevent fraud and undervaluation of declared imports.

Art objects, antiques, and other special imports also come under Customs scrutiny. Customs is charged with the responsibility of determining the value of all imported purchases, no matter how esoteric, as well as helping to prevent the importation of stolen art treasures. These activities require considerable expertise in a wide variety of areas.
Courtesy The Port of New York Authority.

One recent example was a case involving a television component manufacturing company that was charged with commingling foreign and domestic TV tuners, resulting in the loss of $1,755,000 in customs revenue. The penalties collected for this case alone exceeded $2 million for the general treasury.

In the Miami Field Office of the Customs Office of Investigations, it was learned that cut flowers imported from South America were being undervalued by representing them as originating in Puerto Rico, which is part of the United States and whose products are not dutiable. There was an estimated loss of revenue of $250,000. The offending importers were charged with civil fraud violations. They were tried, convicted, and heavily fined.

Fraud against the treasury has, according to an official Treasury document, virtually become routine operating procedure in international commerce. Commercial importing firms, both large and small, determined to reduce their "overhead" costs, have been busy picking the pockets of the American taxpayer. Sometimes the lengths to which producer-exporters and middleman-importers will go in their efforts to evade paying duty are incomprehensible. Not too long ago, a European exporter claimed to be producing pure apple juice and exporting it in large quantities to the United States, the Federal Republic of Germany, and Sweden. Customs fraud investigators made the curious discovery that more apple juice was being exported than the country was capable of producing. They also learned that the producer was importing more grape juice extract than the entire population of that country consumed. The riddle was solved when it was established that the exported apple juice was adulterated with grape extract, depriving Uncle Sam of an estimated $200,000 in customs duties by misclassifying it to avoid duties of 25¢ per gallon.

Responding to the escalation of commercial fraud—not considered to be in the same category as narcotic trafficking—here Customs officials recently ordered that more than half of all the agency's investigative man-hours be devoted to anti-fraud work.

When smuggled or undeclared merchandise is seized by Customs and is neither held as evidence nor returned as stolen property, it is usually auctioned off. This is the annual Customs auction in Houston in 1965, which attracted over 1200 bidders. These annual auctions occur in various regions of the country.

To groom special agents in the art of fraud-hunting, they receive special training. Some actually go to work in the fiscal offices of large corporations, where they observe and even participate in operations. Businessmen, bankers, attorneys, accountants, have been helpful in devising detection techniques and new approaches. The work is done in close cooperation with other federal, state, and metropolitan agencies. Civil fraud actions that entail administrative penalties and/or forfeiture of merchandise constitute 98 percent of fraud cases. The remaining 2 percent consist of criminal prosecution with possible prison terms and criminal fines.

The Office of Investigations at Customs headquarters estimates that 75 percent of all U.S. "twin plant" operations of assembling and processing goods partly in the United States and partly in Mexican, Hong Kong, Singapore, and Taiwan

While ships are still under construction, Customs officers will often measure the dimensions of the holds and storage areas to obtain accurate data on just how much cargo the vessel can carry, and this information is valuable in verifying import declarations.
Courtesy of the National Steel and Shipbuilding Company.

factories have violated the provisions of the Tariff Schedule of the United States of America. Several corporations have been indicted and are awaiting prosecution in what promises to be years of litigation.

Another popular form of fraud is considered "genteel" thievery, such as over-stating nondutiable charges, as when an importer deducts inflated insurance costs and international freight handling charges from the total price he paid; quota violations, when documents are falsified to avoid limitations on the volume of imports authorized; omission of dutiable services and products; and falsification of invoices.

Rarely are two fraud cases alike. There are few precedents to go by. Importation of goods into the United States, the world's richest marketplace, results in endless new importers, new forms and records and methods for keeping them, new correspondence and computerized bookkeeping systems. Despite these obstacles, the number of Customs fraud cases handled in recent years has vastly increased. The total received in penalties in 1974 alone was three-quarters of a *billion* dollars and is expected to double in 1975.

Paid informants are turning over more leads than ever these days. They usually are competitors who have been burned, who are suffering from the recession and inflation, and whose profit margins have been shaved. Sometimes importers turn informant in order to recoup Customs penalties they have had to pay. An informer can collect 25 percent of the value of recovered merchandise from any enforcement agency of the U.S. government, but not more than $50,000, provided he meets the appropriate conditions.

Though the nation's railroad system has not fared well in recent years, a great many imports still enter this country by train, especially along the Canadian border. Customs must still maintain a staff of inspectors trained in the problems of railroad cargo examination.

Protecting the Treasury against fraud is only one of many functions, bewildering in their complexity, coming within the purview of the Customs Service. More than forty laws on the statute books, federal and some state, are enforced by Customs, although the original legislation was sponsored by other government agencies.

Some unusual examples of such enforcement functions are the foreign assets control restrictions for a division of the Treasury Department; collection of excise taxes and the regulation of imported alcoholic beverages for the Internal Revenue Service; control of fissionable materials for the Atomic Energy Commission; dual and multiple screening programs in cooperation with the Public Health Service, the Immigration Service, and the Agriculture Inspection Service; enforcement against pier pilferage for the Federal Bureau of Investigation; and enforcement of the copyright, trademark, and patent restrictions of the Department of Commerce and the Library of Congress.

One of the most dramatic and hazardous of these activities is enforcement of the Neutrality Act, under which the import and export of arms and ammunition is prohibited without State Department licensing. The clandestine shipment of arms to Cuba in the fifties and sixties, to Northern Ireland in the seventies, and to other arms-hungry areas, has consumed much time and effort by Customs officers working on global assignment. The looting of military hardware and its transportation between the United States and foreign nations has become a major challenge to this country, to its law enforcement agencies in general, and to the Customs Service in particular. Illicit traffickers in stolen American grenades, automatic rifles, machine guns, and so on are being paid off in heroin, cocaine, and other narcotics, thus aggravating the problem. Along the United States–Mexican border from San Ysidro to El Paso and farther west, narcotics dealers are currently demanding payment, not in dollars, but in rifles and machine guns.

Thirty-four assorted rifles and automatic weapons, along with 1,500 rounds of ammunition, were seized recently by Customs at Los Angeles International Airport, and after nine weeks of investigation three individuals were arrested. The export of weapons and munitions without a proper license is a violation of the Mutual Security Act of 1954.

Returning armed forces personnel are not exempt from Customs inspection. Under a special "pre-clearance" program, Customs inspectors arrive aboard this navy cruiser while it is still at sea to speed up the inspection process.

Customs personnel are deployed throughout the United States and its territorial possessions, and offices are also maintained in the capitals of the principal countries of Europe, Southeast Asia, and the Far East. Each of these foreign offices is under the supervision of a Customs attaché or representative who is responsible for ascertaining and verifying market values in the country of origin, and transmitting this information to Washington. Inspectors working at ports of entry base their duty calculations on the data they receive from their associates in foreign capitals.

Customs inspectors are what might be termed the "shock troops" of the service. It is they who meet international travelers on their arrival at ports of entry. They must examine all baggage brought into the country and determine whether the requirements of the law have been fulfilled. In the performance of this duty they are expected to exercise care and tact. It is essential that inspectors have a detailed knowledge of all classes of merchandise that they are required to handle. Today, with the enormously complex changes in rates of duty brought about by foreign trade agreements, the role of the inspector assumes greater importance than ever.

The officers on the Canadian and Mexican borders, once known as Customs border patrol inspectors, are carefully selected. They supplement the regular Customs inspectors at border ports. Their duties expose them to abuse, violence, and even death. They must be ready for all types of emergencies and, although never the aggressors with law violators, they are frequently forced into serious confrontations with hardened criminals engaged in smuggling.

Perhaps more depends upon the import specialists, who appraise and examine merchandise, than upon any other group of Customs employee. Their job is to protect domestic industry and obtain the revenue from imports to which the government is legally entitled. These officers examine samples of every import. It is also their duty to help prevent, so far as may be possible, the smuggling of contraband and the illegal importation of merchandise, of whatever character, into the United States.

The commissioner, who serves as the administrative head of the service, directs a staff of attorneys, administrative officers, and support personnel, who constitute the nerve center of the agency in Washington. Until 1927, the agency was known as a Division of Customs within the Department of Treasury. For forty-six years it was known as a bureau, until its name was changed to the United States Customs Service, by order of Secretary of the Treasury George P. Shultz. The change restored its original name and emphasized its policy of public service.

The United States Customs officer has been protecting the American people on the land, in the air, at sea, along the Mexican and Canadian borders, at inland ports and the Great Lakes, the seaways and the Gulf Coast, since 1789.

This is the Customs story.

chapter two

The Tariff System from Ancient Times to Colonial America

One of the early meanings of *custom* was the money or services rendered by a feudal tenant to his lord, or the obligation to give or the right to receive this. The collection of tribute was already an established practice in the deepest recesses of antiquity. As soon as the swords of nations had opened the travel lanes of the world, caravans laden with local wares began to crisscross the globe. The earliest recorded history reveals trade among nations by barter and collectors who were known to accept a portion of these goods in payment of tolls. With the first minting of coins and the creation of money, commerce and exchange became much easier, as did the collection of tariffs, resulting in the great enrichment of monarchs.

As early as Old Testament times, custom was recognized as an important source of income, and the right to collect it as a form of political control as effective as outright slavery. After Cyrus of Persia had permitted the captive Israelites to return from Babylon to Jerusalem to rebuild the city and temple, there were those in the land who "weakened the hands of the people of Judah, and troubled them in building, and hired counsellors against them, to frustrate their purpose." To King Artaxerxes, who reigned later, these people declared:

> Be it known now unto the king, that, if this city be builded, and the walls set up again, then they will not pay toll, tribute, and custom . . . (Ezra 4:13)

All building was stopped. First King Darius and then another Artaxerxes succeeded to the throne. The second King Artaxerxes restored the Hebrew state and decreed that "it shall not be lawful to impose tribute, custom, or toll upon the priests and Levites, the signers, porters, or ministers of this house of God."

The New Testament records that Jesus called Matthew from "the receipt of customs." Matthew doubtless was a collector of tolls and customs duties at the Sea of Galilee. Matthew is also referred to as a publican, or tax gatherer. Paul, in addressing the Romans, advised them to "render custom to whom custom is due."

During the violent clashes that took place in the early history of the struggle between the English kings and Parliament over the levying and disposition of taxes, the kings claimed that money received from "ancient customs" was rightfully theirs and that Parliament had no jurisdiction over it. The implication was that the Crown was entitled to this source of income by "right" or "custom."

During the feudal period, favored barons were given a special privilege to levy taxes. Those who imported foreign merchandise or sold certain domestic commodities were taxed for the right to trade by lords or barons under special grants from the king. One baron would have the exclusive right to levy tribute on salt, while another would be granted the privilege for some other commodity. These lords grew rich on customs and were thus able to support their retainers and contribute to the wars of their kings.

The kings, by "divine right," levied taxes upon these feudal lords, sometimes referred to as robber barons. The kings had the authority to raise revenue by levying taxes on the feudal lords, to raise armed forces to sustain their orders, to punish recalcitrants, and to conquer other nobles and kings, bringing them into their spheres of influence and increasing their tribute.

The word *tariff* was coined in a climate of bloodshed and plunder. It all began in a little town called Tarifa on the coast of Spain, near Gibraltar. Like Gibraltar, Tarifa is located on a high promontory, linked to the mainland only by a narrow, easily defended causeway. Twelve centuries ago, when the Moors founded Tarifa, they pioneered a system that changed the course of economic history.

As international commerce spread from country to country, a predatory group of pirates made the strategically located town of Tarifa their command post. From this point they held up merchant vessels, levying tribute according to a fixed scale on all merchandise passing in or out of the straits. Mariners who reluctantly paid tribute at Tarifa soon began calling the tribute a "tariff," and the word entered common usage in England, since English vessels dominated the seas in burgeoning international commerce. It was only a matter of time before the word was taken up by the sea traders—by the Spanish and Portuguese (*tarifa*), the French (*tarife* or *tarif*), and the Italian (*tariffa*).

The governments of Europe, not loath to pick up a good idea, began making similar levies on imports, and tariffs became a valuable source of revenue. A sophisticated tariff system was fairly well established in the Old World when the American colonies were founded.

A tax on goods was in fact the most common source of revenue among the civilized nations of the Old World. The early Greeks had a highly developed system of tolls, both for imports and exports, while the more advanced Athenians exacted fees from foreign vessels anchoring in Greek harbors. During the Middle Ages the feudal lords imposed a charge on everything that passed through their provinces, dotting the whole of Europe with customhouses—every river crossing and entrance to larger cities had its collectors of customs.

One of the earliest recorded mentions of port tax collecting in the English-speaking world is found in the Code of Laws enacted by King Ethelred, in A.D. 979:

> Every small vessel arriving at Billingsgate shall pay to the tax gatherer one oblus [the equivalent of one penny and a farthing]; if of greater tonnage and mast rigged, one denarius [seven and a half pence]. If a ship shall arrive and anchor there, four denarii shall be paid to the tax gatherer. Vessels laden with timber shall pay one log to the tax gatherer.

Billingsgate was believed to be the first port of entry in the United Kingdom. Duty was imposed on timber and was payable in kind. So outraged were the merchants that they hurled epithets and vile curses at the customs collectors. The word billingsgate assumed the meaning it has when King Ethelred ruled England.

American practices are deeply rooted in the centuries of tradition created by the Customs and Excise officers of the mother country, England.

Although the pattern of Britain's toll system up to the twelfth century is indistinct in the blur of the long-forgotten past, we know that before the middle of the eighth century, the king granted to the bishop of London part of his customs tribute.

The offices of the collector of customs trace back to the time of the Winchester Assize, a document issued 1203/4, known as "the Customs of the Realm of England." It was an effort on the part of the Crown to centralize collections and replace an older, more loosely run system that had resulted in a significant loss of revenue.

The Winchester Assize was the foundation of the English medieval customs administration. It contained some of the basic elements of our modern assessment, collection, and accounting systems. Entry papers covering seaboard trade, both foreign and coastwise, began at this time to include a description of the goods, the date of shipment, and the name of the merchant.

In 1215, the Magna Charta referred to the collection of customs as a basic and lawful right of the governing authority. A century and a half later the poet Geoffrey Chaucer was appointed Comptroller of the Port of London to work in Tronage Hall, known as the "weighhouse," with the scale and weights of the King's Beam. The "computatorium" was on the second floor, with the cellars or warehouse below.

The layout of the early customhouses was the pattern for customhouse construction for years afterward. The computatorium was renamed the "Long Room" by Sir Christopher Wren, architect of many of England's most famous buildings and churches, including St. Paul's Cathedral, and this style, well established by the year 1700, can be found in twentieth-century America. The famous customhouse at Salem, Massachusetts, where the novelist Nathaniel Hawthorne served

The London Custom House built in 1671 by
Sir Christopher Wren, architect of St. Paul's
Cathedral, after the Great Fire of London
in 1666.
Courtesy of H. M. Customs & Excise.

Wren's Custom House was itself destroyed
by fire in 1714, and this building took its
place.
Courtesy of H. M. Customs & Excise.

as a Customs employee, was modeled after the customhouse of Norfolk, England.

In 1297 the British enacted what we would regard as a liberal "Statute Concerning Tilliage." The royal proclamation read:

No Tilliage or Aid shall be taken or levied by us or our Heirs in our Realm, without the good will and Assent of the Archbishops, Bishops, Earls, Barons, Knights, Burgesses and other Freemen of the Land. No officer of ours, or of our Heirs, shall take Corn, Leather, Cattle or any other Goods of any manner of Person, without the good will and assent of the Party to Whom the Goods belongs.

In 1311 it was decreed that all officers of the Customs must be English born.

Forasmuch as it was heretofore ordained that the Customs of the Realm should be received and kept by the People of the Realm and not by Aliens; and that the Issues and Profits of the same Customs, together with all other Issues and Profits of the Realm arising, whatsoever they be, should come entirely into the King's Exchequer, and by the Treasurer and Chamberlain be received and delivered for the maintenance of the King's Household, and otherwise to his profit, so that the King might live on his own, without making prices other than those anciently due and rightful; the which matters are not observed—Wherefore We do ordain that the same Customs, together with all the Issues of the Realm as afore is said, be received and kept by the People of the Realm and delivered into the Exchequer in the form aforementioned.

In 1323 another statute "for Estreats of the Exchequer" was enacted, providing that the Butler to the King "should have all his purchases." It was the first regulation giving Customs officers a title: "Gatherers of the King's Customs" or "Customers." It read:

Witnessed by the view of the honestest men of the Town where the Purveyance shall happen, and if it happened that the same be in a Port where are Gatherers of the King's Customs the same shall be testified by them.
[Then it added:] And no Customer from henceforth shall be deputed to the Butler, so long as he shall be attendant upon the Customs. . . . And all the Customers of England shall be charged according as they are assigned for the gathering of Custom within certain bounds, that they twice yearly shall certify the Treasurer and Barons, that is to say at the XV of Easter of St. Michael, how many ships have arrived within their Bounds within that time loaden with Wines, and of whence they were, and who brought them, and when they arrived and discharged, and how much Wine every Ship did bring, etc., how many ships have arrived of which the King did take Prise of Wine and how many Tuns, and in what Ships the King did take two shillings for the Tun, and no other Prise, and how many Tuns he did take Two shillings for the Tun, and also other Prise.

The royal purse was thus protected by the imposition of customs duty based on the tonnage of each ship and also on the cargo it carried. The tax on wine became a fixed tradition which has never been rescinded.

As early as 1388 conflict of interest was banned: "That no Customer or Comptroller should be appointed for gifts" and "That no Customer nor Comptroller have any Ships of their own, nor meddle with the Freight of Ships . . . and that no Customer, Comptroller, Searcher, Weigher, or Finder shall have any such office for Term of Life, but so long as it shall please the King."

The first known mention of the title "collector" can be found in a 1393 statute fixing the tenure of office in Customs.

It is ordained and established: That no Searcher, Gauger of Mines, Aulneger [finder] nor Weigher of Wools or any other Merchandise, Collectors of Customs or Subsidies whatsoever, or Comptroller shall have estate in his office for Term of Life, or of Years; but that the said offices shall remain in the King's Hands under the Governance of the Treasurer for the Time being, with the Assent of the Council, where Need is; and if any Charters or Letters Patent be made on the contrary, they shall be clearly annulled, void and of none Effect.

The same statute decreed that "Customers" render sworn accounts; the Collector continued to be known as the *Customer* until the reign of Charles II.

The first customhouse in the colonies, built in 1706, in Yorktown, Virginia.

A facsimile of a weekly newspaper printed in Providence just a few years before the American Revolution. In the lower right column is a complaint by Colonial Customs officials to the British government that, because of the mood of the Boston citizenry, they cannot obtain adequate military protection to continue to collect taxes.

[Vol. VI.]   THE   [Numb. 298.]

PROVIDENCE GAZETTE;

AND COUNTRY JOURNAL.

Containing the freſheſt AD- VICES, Foreign and Domeſtic

From SATURDAY, September 16, to SATURDAY, September 23, 1769.

Printed by JOHN CARTER, near the COURT-HOUSE.

PROVIDENCE.

The following Bill having paſſed the Lower Houſe of Aſſembly, at September Seſſion, by a conſiderable Majority, now reſts before the Upper Houſe for Conſideration—and 'tis thought will paſs that Houſe alſo.

An ACT for the more equal Diſtribution of Inteſtate Eſtates.

WHEREAS Reaſon and Equity plainly point out, that the Eſtate of a Parent who dies inteſtate ſhould be divided among all his Children in an equitable Proportion, unleſs where ſome political Conſiderations may make a contrary Method more ſuitable to the Circumſtances and Conſtitution of a Country; none of which Reaſons do at preſent, nor can for a long Time exiſt in this Colony: And whereas many and great Inconveniences and Diſadvantages are by long Experience found to ariſe from the preſent Mode in which inteſtate Eſtates deſcend in this Colony;

Be it therefore Enacted by this General Aſſembly, and by the Authority thereof it is Enacted, That where any Perſon ſhall die inteſtate, leaving Lands in this Colony, in which ſuch Inteſtate had an Eſtate in Fee Simple, the Fee and Eſtate in ſuch Lands ſhall ſeparate and deſcend to, and be divided amongſt, and veſt in, all the Children of ſuch Inteſtate in Fee Simple, in the following Manner, that is to ſay, the whole of ſuch Lands ſhall be divided into a Number of Shares or Portions, exceeding by one the Number of ſuch Inteſtate's Children; two of which Shares or Portions ſhall deſcend to, veſt in, and belong to, the eldeſt Son of ſuch Inteſtate, and one Share or Portion ſhall deſcend to, veſt in, and belong to, each of the other Children of ſuch Inteſtate.

And be it further Enacted by the Authority aforeſaid, That where any Perſon ſeized and poſſeſſed of any real Eſtate in Fee Simple, ſhall die inteſtate as aforeſaid, leaving no Sons, but ſeveral Daughters, in that Caſe ſuch real Eſtate ſhall deſcend to all the Daughters in equal Proportion.

And be it further Enacted by the Authority aforeſaid, That if any Perſon ſeized and poſſeſſed of any real Eſtate in Fee Simple, ſhall die inteſtate, and leave no Children, in that Caſe ſuch real Eſtate ſhall deſcend to, veſt in, and be divided amongſt, the next of Kin, in equal Shares and Proportions, and in Fee Simple; and that where any Perſon who by this Act would have been intitled to a Share or Portion in any ſuch Inteſtate's real Eſtate, if he or ſhe had ſurvived the Inteſtate, ſhall die before the Inteſtate, and leave legal Repreſentatives, in every ſuch Caſe, ſuch Repreſentatives ſhall receive and hold the ſame Share or Portion of ſuch real Eſtate in Fee Simple, as the Perſon would have done whom they ſhall repreſent, in caſe he or ſhe had ſurvived the Inteſtate; and that ſuch Repreſentatives ſhall take in the ſame Manner and Proportion as directed in the firſt Paragraph of this Act.

Provided neverthelefs, and the true Intent and Meaning hereof is, That no Perſon ſhall be intitled to and receive a double Portion of the real Eſtate of any Perſon who ſhall die inteſtate as aforeſaid, excepting only the eldeſt Son of ſuch Inteſtate, or the Repreſentative of ſuch eldeſt Son.

Provided alſo, That no Diſtribution of any real Eſtate, in Conſequence of this Act, ſhall extend to, or be made in the collateral Line, beyond the Brothers and Siſters of ſuch Inteſtate, and their Children, and to thoſe only of the whole Blood.

And be it further Enacted by the Authority aforeſaid, That when the Children of any Perſon who ſhall die inteſtate ſhall receive from their Parent Deeds of Gift of Lands, or other real Eſtate, for their Advancement in the World, or for Marriage Portions, that in the Settlement of ſuch Parent's Eſtate dying inteſtate, the ſame ſhall be conſidered as Part of their Dividend of ſuch real Eſtate, and if it ſhall not amount to a full Proportion thereof, that they ſhall be intitled to and receive ſo much more as will make them equal to the other Perſons intitled to a Part of

ſuch real Eſtate, agreeable to this Act, unleſs where the Parent who makes the Gift ſhall, in doing the ſame, expreſly declare, that the ſame is not given as Part of their Portion.

And be it further Enacted, That in caſe of any poſthumous Child or Children, the ſame be intitled to, and ſhall inherit in the ſame Manner as though born before the Death of their Inteſtate.

Provided neverthelefs, and be it further Enacted by the Authority aforeſaid, That nothing in this Act contained ſhall extend, or be conſtrued to extend, to deprive the Widow of any Perſon dying inteſtate of her Right of Dower, as ſhe now by Law is intitled to.

And be it Enacted by the Authority aforeſaid, That for the equal Diviſion of ſuch inteſtate Eſtate, it ſhall and may be lawful for any or either of the Heirs of ſuch Eſtate to apply, by himſelf or Guardian, if a Minor, by Petition or Writ of Partition, to the Inferior or Superior Courts in and for the County where ſuch Eſtate lies, for a Diviſion of ſuch Eſtate; and that ſuch Court ſhall thereupon iſſue Citation (if by Petition) to each and every of ſuch Heirs, or their Guardians, to appear before ſaid Court at a certain Day, to join in ſuch Diviſion, when and where it ſhall be lawful for ſuch Heirs, by themſelves or Guardians, to enter into a Rule of Court, thereby ſubmitting ſuch Diviſion to three Men or more, to be choſen by them, and allowed by ſaid Court for that Purpoſe, who ſhall make Report to the ſame Court how they have divided the ſame; and which Report, when accepted, and Judgment entered thereon, ſhall be binding upon all Parties; and the Coſt and Charge thereupon be paid equally by all ſuch Heirs: But in caſe ſuch Rule cannot be agreed upon, that then it ſhall and may be lawful for ſuch Court to order a ſpecial Jury to be empannelled for dividing ſuch Eſtate, who ſhall make Diviſion thereof, and make Return of the ſame to ſuch Court, and Judgment being entered thereon, the ſame to be final, and the Coſt and Charge thereof ſhall be paid equally by ſuch Heirs.

And in caſe any Diſpute ſhall ariſe between Perſons claiming a Diviſion of ſuch Eſtate, that then a Trial at the ſame Court ſhall be had between ſuch Perſons before ſaid Court, agreeable to Law, before ſuch Diviſion be made; and one Trial before ſuch Court ſhall be final.

And be it further Enacted, That in caſe any Action or Suit ſhall be brought for any Debt or Demand due from ſuch Inteſtate, the ſame ſhall be brought againſt all thoſe who take and inherit the real Eſtates of ſuch Inteſtates, if to be found, and Executions ſhall be ſerved upon, and the Debts or Damages and Coſts recovered, levied and collected, from or out of the Eſtates of the ſeveral Heirs of ſuch Inteſtates, in the ſame Proportion as they inherit, if ſuch real Eſtates remain unalienated, and can conveniently be ſo done. And in caſe the ſame be levied in any other Proportion, that then the Parties aggrieved thereby ſhall be intitled to an Action, and recover of any Perſon or Perſons in Arrears all ſuch Arrearages, with Coſts.

The Subject of a MARKET-HOUSE in Providence continued.

THE advantages which muſt reſult both to the ſeller and buyer, by means of a market-houſe, are very plain, if we conſider, that in our preſent mode of getting the daily proviſions for a family, both parties muſt go after each other.—A great deal of time muſt be ſpent by each, and when they meet the price is unſettled; whereas if there was a ſtated place to ſell and buy, the market price would be eaſily aſcertained. In ſuch caſe the market man would not aſk more than the fixed price, and the buyer would be quickly diſpatched, and carry home his proviſions. When a man, who lives at the extremity of the town, meets with what he wants near home, he muſt either give an advanced price, or dog the market man half a day about town, until he comes down to the current price of the article in queſtion.

When a countryman brings for ſale meat, butter, cheeſe, or any other ſorts of proviſions, he generally at firſt aſks too much, and what the market will not bear: However, thinking that the inhabitants want to impoſe upon him, he perſiſts in his demand, and carries his articles about town until the inhabitants have contrived a ſupply; and then he is reduced to this dilemma, either to carry the things home, or ſell them at half price. There are always to be found perſons enough in a great town, who would take the advantage of ſuch market people, eſpecially if they diſcover their unſkilfulneſs in marketing, to the great diſcouragement of the country.

The inconvenience of calling at every door, anſwering queſtions, diſputing about the price, the fatigues of heat, cold, rain and ſnow, joined to the damage which the proviſions muſt ſuffer by being carried about, is enough to convince the country, as well as the town, that a market-houſe would be of ſingular advantage to both.

If it ſhould be objected, that the eſtabliſhment of a regular market would tend to bring on a caſh trade inſtead of truck for proviſions, I anſwer, that would be a mighty bleſſing indeed, inſtead of a diſadvantage. In ſuch caſe the merchant or employer would be obliged to pay the tradeſman or labourer as much more caſh in proportion, as the new regulation in the affair of marketing ſhould make it neceſſary for him to expend. And in ſuch caſe, the market man would lay out caſh in town for all ſuch articles as he wanted to be ſupplied with. There never was a good market where Truck was the word; and thoſe who would diſcourage the building a public market from a truck principle, are blind to their own intereſt, that of the public, and of poſterity.

After all, the market man might have his election, either to go about town, or ſell at the market, unleſs ſome future regulation ſhould reſtrain him.

A. B.

From the BOSTON EVENING-POST.

MEMORIALS of the Commiſſioners of the Cuſtoms in North-America, with ſeveral Letters and Papers annexed.

May it pleaſe your Lordſhips,

IN our former memorials to your Lordſhips, we repreſented the diſaffection of the people here to the revenue laws, and from the many treaſonable publications that had been ſpread through all the provinces, and the correſpondence carried on by the ſeveral aſſemblies, we were perſuaded there had been a long concerted and extenſive plan of reſiſtance to the authority of Great-Britain; and we believe, that the ſeizure referred to in the incloſed papers, has haſtened the people of Boſton to the commiſſion of actual violence ſooner than was intended.

From their outrageous behaviour towards our officers, and their repeated threats of immediate violence to our own perſons, we found it abſolutely neceſſary, in order to ſave his Majeſty's commiſſion from further inſult, and to preſerve our lives, to take ſhelter on board his Majeſty's ſhip the Romney, in Boſton harbour, from whence we are removed into Caſtle-William, to carry on the buſineſs of the revenue, till we can receive ſuch protection as will enable us to act with ſafety at Boſton.

We herewith lay before your Lordſhips copies of our minutes of the 13th and 14th inſt. together with copies of ſeveral affidavits and letters relative to our preſent ſituation, agreeable to the ſchedule incloſed, and we beg leave to ſubmit our opinion, that nothing but the immediate exertion of military power will prevent an open revolt of this town, which may probably ſpread throughout the provinces. Which is humbly ſubmitted.

Caſtle-William, HENRY HULTON,
Boſton Harbour, JOHN TEMPLE,
June 16, 1768. WILLIAM BURCH,
 CHARLES PAXTON,
 JOHN ROBINSON.

The origin of the term Naval Officer, an official of the Customs Service in the nineteenth century, has been traced back to 1660 when an act was passed by Parliament that restricted trade in and with the Plantations and Colonies to English ships, commanded by English officers, and manned by English subjects. Under this provision, an officer was appointed by each colonial governor whose special duty it was to enforce the navigation laws and secure the prerequisites of the king and governor by forfeiture. "And whereas by the said Act . . . the Governors of the said Plantations are impowered to appoint an officer for the Performance of certain things in the Act mentioned, which said Officer is there commonly known by the name of the Naval Officer."

An act passed in 1672 imposed duty upon certain goods shipped to the American plantations, and an English Board of Commissioners of Customs was established to enforce it and generally control the economic problems which the Act brought in its wake. The commissioners never could have won a popularity contest; indeed, they became the focal point for much of the pent-up anger and hostility the colonial peoples felt for the Crown. Customs representatives were sent across the Atlantic with commissions from the Board. They had the "Power to enter any ship, bottom, boat or other vessel" and "to enter into any house, shop, cellar, warehouse or other place whatsoever, not only within the said port but within any other port or place" within their jurisdiction, "there to make diligent search, and in case of resistance to break open any drawer, trunk, chest . . . or other parcel or package whatsoever for any goods, wares, or merchandise prohibited to be exported out or imported into said port," or for which "the customs or other duties had not been fully paid."

Three centuries later, the United States Customs Service still exercises a similar search authority. Enforcement of the prohibition on certain goods has had priority over the collection of duty, signifying that the controls placed on trade were considered even more important than the amounts of money realized. At many American ports, during the colonial period the amount of duty collected was often insufficient to defray the cost of salaries. The commissioners in England drew up a code of instruction for the colonial officials, and trained their own officials and even the governors of provinces on how the rigorous customs laws and regulations were to be applied.

Later in the colonial period a Board was established in Boston to handle the American customs business along the continental seaboard from Newfoundland to Bermuda. It was accountable to the Receiver General in London for all duties collected. Under the supervision of the Boston Board, the collectors were doing business in Plymouth, Salem, Marblehead, Rhode Island, New London, New Haven, New York, Philadelphia, Chester, Patapsco, Potomac, the James River, upper and lower Mobile, Rappahannock, Beaufort, Charleston, Brunswick, Savannah, the York River, and Pensacola.

The salaries of these port officials were so low that they were allowed to supplement them "by receipts of incidents." Occasionally certain officers served with no official salary at all, siphoning off their reimbursement from seizures, penalties, and "merchants' fees."

Facsimiles of early English bills of lading,
which were used as written evidence of a
contract for delivery of goods sent by sea.
Courtesy of the British Public Record Office.

A colonial staff list for the Port of Boston in 1779 shows that Edward Winslow, a port official at Plymouth, and others, served without official pay. A New York staff list shows that the "weighers" (responsible for determining and assessing duty on all dry goods taxed by weight) and the "gaugers" (those who looked after the wet goods taxed by measure or volume) received no salary, but an "allowance" of sixpence per weighed cask and threepence per cask of liquid measure. Another port official was listed as the "Surveyor and Searcher." The job of searcher, also known as the "medieval scrutator," had its origins in the time of Richard II in the 1380s and is the equivalent of the modern Customs inspector. In 1776, London Customs Museum documents record that Joseph Harrison was in office as the colonial collector of the Port of Boston, with an annual salary of

£100. This office and the staff of searchers, tidesmen, surveyors, weighers, and gaugers played an important part in the eventual growth of the U.S. Customs Service.

The Old Custom House in Boston.

The Custom House in Boston today.

chapter three

Customs and the American Nation

The "imbalance of payments" that plagues us today is nothing new. For seventy-five years before the American Revolution, the annual trade balance was against the American colonies and heavily in favor of Britain. By 1754 the colonies were one million dollars in the red. By 1760, they had imported more than they had exported to the extent of nine million dollars, not a large amount by today's standards, but in 1760 a fortune. Furthermore, English currency in circulation in the colonies was in short supply. The merchants and moneylenders of London demanded cash to resolve past indebtedness, with the result that the colonies were pinched for the exchange they needed for ordinary business transactions.

Lord Cornwallis surrendered in 1781, and his troops marched out of Yorktown, Virginia, to a tune called "The World Turned Upside Down." The Revolution ended officially in 1783 with the signing of the Treaty of Paris. From then until 1789, the country was not a nation, but a group of squabbling independent states under the Articles of Confederation, each suspicious and jealous of the others.

The most immediate problem to be solved by the new nation was the problem of foreign debts—French and Dutch—inherited from an improvident Confederation that had run up bills without any plan for repayment, and on which it had not even paid interest.

The government was saddled with $12 million of foreign debts and another $40 million in domestic debts, including $13 million in unpaid interest alone.

The war debts of the individual states brought the total up to a staggering $81 million.

When it came to taxation, the Continental government was a pleading pauper. Congress did not have the power to levy taxes directly. Instead, it made requisitions on the recalcitrant states in proportion to the assessed value of their land, but the necessary enforcement muscle wasn't there. At one point, the Treasury did not have a dollar in the till.

The government needed $9 million. Congress hoped to raise $4 million in loans, and state treasuries were asked to contribute $5 million. They came up with only $442,000, with the Carolinas, Georgia, and Delaware refusing to give anything. When Congress tried to issue bonds or certificates of indebtedness, they promptly depreciated, with nothing in back of them but a promise and vague hopes for a brighter future. Every state had a different set of tariff laws and some states had set up tariff barriers against each other.

Congress had no legislative power over individuals. Its legislation applied only to the states; federal codes of civil or criminal law were nonexistent. Any public jurisdiction could issue paper money and did. Each state and even each bank had its own currency. Congress issued Continental money. Besides a bewildering variety of local currencies, a great deal of foreign money was also in circulation. Only metal coins held their value. The expression "not worth a continental" is a grim reminder of prevailing conditions in the money market in eighteenth-century America.

There was no letup in the bickering among the states. The causes of discord were often so trivial as to make the disputes seem incomprehensible. The row between New York, Connecticut, and New Jersey is an example. The New York legislature came to the conclusion that too much money was going from New York City into the pockets of Connecticut Yankees and Jersey men. Connecticut supplied most of New York's firewood, and the farmers of New Jersey sent boatloads of vegetables, chickens, and eggs across the Hudson to New York. So New York placed a heavy duty on these products. Every chicken peddler from New Jersey had to take his fowl to the customhouse, have them valued, obtain clearance papers, and pay duty. Eggs were counted and hens were weighed. Connecticut firewood was measured; cabbages were appraised. Duties had to be paid on everything.

New Jersey residents rose in wrath. The City of New York owned a lighthouse on Sandy Hook. The New Jersey legislature levied a tax of $1,800 a year on it. Connecticut merchants decided to boycott New York. They formed an association and bound themselves, under penalties, not to buy or sell in the city.

Foreign mercantilism was also a problem. In 1783 the British Government proclaimed that all cargoes in the West Indian trade must be carried in British ships. In retaliation New York laid a double duty on goods imported in British vessels, while Massachusetts, New Hampshire, and Rhode Island prohibited British ships from carrying cargoes out of their harbors. Connecticut took thrifty advantage of the situation. She threw her ports open, duty free, to British commerce, to the dismay of her neighbors, following it up with tariffs on all goods coming into Connecticut from Massachusetts.

Other states, too, refused to cooperate with each other. Maryland claimed the entire width of the Potomac River as part of her state territory. Her learned men, assisted by others not so learned, contended on the strength of antique charters that a vessel at a wharf on the Virginia shore of the Potomac was in Maryland territory. Virginia ridiculed the assertion and, in turn, tried to collect fees from every vessel entering Chesapeake Bay on the grounds that she owned the light-houses on both sides of the mouth of the Chesapeake. The matter was adjusted only after much vituperation and bitterness, extensively reported in the contemporary press.

During the crucial formative years between 1776 and 1781, all the states, with the single exception of Virginia, had either failed or neglected to fully enforce their tariff acts. Economic conditions were chaotic. Merchants were complaining bitterly and distribution of consumer goods was sporadic. Strong action and leadership were needed, and soon.

Pennsylvania had never collected much revenue from duties on imported merchandise, and, for several years after the Declaration of Independence, Maryland had no collector of customs at all. The end of the Revolution found the states on the edge of bankruptcy, and they began to reimpose old abandoned duties, raise the rates, and add to the lists of merchandise to be appraised and taxed. The tariff situation between 1784 and 1789 was, to put it mildly, a patchquilt of laws, lacking any uniformity.

Virginia maintained her import duties during the hectic life of the Continental Congress, taxing exported tobacco and imported liquors as her chief source of revenue. In 1785, she added to the amounts of duties and increased the number of articles subject to taxation.

Between 1779 and 1789, Virginia passed more tariff laws than any other state. Connecticut had duties and excise taxes in operation in 1784. A year later rates were increased to 7 percent, but in the main her rates were comparatively low. New Hampshire had fairly high rates that appear to have been imposed to raise revenue and protect home industry. Rhode Island imposed higher rates than New Hampshire, Connecticut, or Virginia and prescribed more stringent administrative features in its tariff bills. In 1785, her legislature passed an act for the levying of additional duties, modeled on the acts of Massachusetts and New York. Massachusetts had prospered commercially during the war when the state pursued a policy of free trade. In 1782 she apologetically imposed a tax on imported goods as a revenue measure, the act to remain in effect "until six months after peace, and no longer." New tariff legislation in 1784 raised duties and another increase took place in 1785 and again in 1786. In comparison with those of other states, the duties of Massachusetts were quite high. In 1784 New York followed in the footsteps of her prosperous neighbor to the east and passed a law based on the Massachusetts act. The methods of collecting duties were eventually incorporated into the legislation of the First Congress, inspired by the law that New York enacted in 1784.

Pennsylvania went about the work of tariff legislation in a slow but sure way. In time her tariff laws became even more stringent than those of Massachusetts. Up to 1780 the state had "free ports," a result of Quaker free-trade influence, but in that year Pennsylvania enacted her first tariff legislation by levying minor duties on imported articles. It appears to have been purely a revenue measure. There was minor tariff legislation in 1782 and 1784, and then, in September 1785, the state passed an act which has been described as the foundation of the country's first Tariff Act of 1789. New Jersey imposed no customs duties, while the southern states, except for Virginia, set up tariffs to raise revenue. The rates were far from uniform in each state and importers were quick to take advantage of the differences.

A convention at Hartford, Connecticut, first urged on the Congress the urgent necessity for a uniform system of commercial regulation. Contemporary journals echo the protests and requests from commercial conventions and individual businessmen. Early in 1784, Congress appointed a committee of five, with Thomas Jefferson as chairman, to consider petitions and letters in relation to commerce and trade. On April 20 of that year, the Committee recommended that the states provide "the United States in Congress assembled for the term of 15 years with a power to prohibit any goods, wares, or merchandise from being imported into any of the States except in vessels belonging to and navigated by citizens of the United States, or the subjects of foreign power with whom the United States has treaties of commerce." Congress approved the recommendation but it had only slight effect on the legislatures of the various states.

Two years later a congressional committee reported that Massachusetts, New York, New Jersey, and Virginia had adopted the recommendation. Connecticut, Pennsylvania, and Maryland endorsed it but deferred the implementation date. Rhode Island had enacted legislation which did not wholly conform with the recommendations. The other states didn't act at all—a graphic illustration of the fact that the federal government had yet to prove that it had the power to govern.

In the early years of the republic, treasury funds were rapidly depleted, public debts were increasing, loans were hard to procure, and the states were slow in honoring requisitions for funds made on them by the central government. The congressional resolution of 1781, requesting authority to levy a tax of 5 percent on all goods imported, to fix rates, and to provide the means for collecting them, had failed. It would have deprived the state authorities of patronage by giving the power of appointment for Customs positions to the federal government. This resolution, had it been adopted, would have given the federal government power to fix rates and provide the machinery for imposing and collecting duties. The consent of all the states to the proposal was needed and the state governors were requested to convene their legislatures and take action on the urgent and dramatic appeal.

A little more than a year after its introduction, all the states except Rhode Island and Georgia agreed to support the idea. Georgia eventually gave approval with necessary legislation, but Rhode Island was adamant in her opposition. A congressional committee visited the state and attempted to impress upon the legislature the gravity of the situation and the fact that the plan would fail unless it was universally adopted. Rhode Island held out, Virginia soon withdrew her consent, and the plan was dead.

Government finances were going from bad to worse, and something had to be done. The imminent loss of political patronage was a big stumbling block and a determined Congress set out to solve the problem. It placed before the states a plan for a uniform 5 percent tax and specific duties on a restricted list of imports. The critical issue of patronage was handled by a concession to the states allowing them to continue to appoint collectors of Customs, with the proviso that they should be under the jurisdiction of and subject to removal by the Congress.

A resolution was adopted by Congress on April 18, 1783, and a committee with James Madison, Alexander Hamilton, and Oliver Ellsworth as members was authorized to present the case to the states. This the committee did in the form of a dramatic address written by the gifted Hamilton, giving reasons for prompt action and meeting the objections raised against the previous plan. The states responded with agonizing slowness. In 1786, nearly three long years later, New York, Georgia, Rhode Island, and Maryland still had not given their consent.

During the spring and summer of that year Georgia, Rhode Island, and Maryland came in with proper legislative enactments. Now it was New York that stayed out, bold and defiant. Congress passed a resolution asking Governor Clinton to convene the legislature in special session to approve the plan. He declined, asserting that under the state constitution he had no power to call an extra session, except for extraordinary business, and this question had already been before the legislature and had been voted down. It was, therefore, in the nature of *res adjudicata*, a closed subject or fait accompli, and he had not the power to call the legislature together to pass on a question it had already discussed in detail and on which it had taken definite action.

The United States floundered along, heavily in debt, with impaired credit, with no source of desperately needed revenue, confronted with quarrelsome states unable or unwilling to face up to the danger inherent in the lack of taxing authority by the infant republic.

The First Tariff Act—July 4, 1789

In a memorable demonstration of democracy at work, simple tradesmen, manufacturers, importers, and ordinary citizens gave voice to their feelings that emergency action was needed to save the country from financial collapse. A petition from Baltimore asked for new legislation that would enable Congress to collect duties on imported merchandise. The petition led to the historic House Bill No. 3 of the First Congress. It was received on April 11, 1789, and was immediately referred to the Committee of the Whole, or a full quorum of the House, in Congress assembled. James Madison, a free trader, proposed the tariff measure as a "temporary expedient" designed to provide the government with desperately needed revenue. Madison had told the House of Representatives: ". . . A national revenue must be obtained; but the system must be such a one that, while it secures the object or revenue, it shall not be oppressive to our constituents. Happy it is for us that such a system is within our powers; for I apprehend that both these objects may be obtained from an impost on objects imported into the United States."

Madison's plan called for a flat 5 percent levy on all imports, but the protectionists, wishing to promote domestic industry, amended the bill to provide higher levies. Duties were assessed on imports of beverages, foods, candles, steel and iron, carriages and harness, footwear, glass, furs, paper, spices, fruits and preserved products.

The debate on the bill was marked by bitter differences between the industrialized North and the agricultural South. In his journal, Senator William Maclay of Pennsylvania described the "log rolling" which preceded passage of the bill in dramatic language.

"My business with Mr. Fitzsimmons this morning," wrote Maclay on May 12, 1789, "was to inform him how much I feared the cabal of New England members in the Senate, and that if they were not gratified in some measure, as to their favorite article of molasses, they would join with every member who objected to any single article and promise him gratification in his particular humor if he would join them. By these means, all the discontents being united and indulgence given, even to caprice and whim, the bill would be lost."

The South demanded protection for tobacco, canned products, hemp, coal, iron, and steel. New England rum distillers wanted free trade in molasses, while Southern producers favored a duty of up to six cents per gallon. Pennsylvania brewers asked for a tax of nine cents per gallon on beer in casks, but wanted beer bottles admitted free. Maryland demanded a glass tax to protect a vital industry. Virginia, which then included West Virginia, sought protection for its coal mines, and tobacco-growing states demanded a duty that "ought to amount to a prohibition."

Madison's resolution of April eighth levying duties on rum and "spiritous liquors," molasses, wines, teas, pepper, sugar, cocoa, and coffee was supplemented by a hundred more articles offered by Representative Fitzsimmons.

It was largely due to the organizing genius of Fitzsimmons, the delegate from Pennsylvania, that eventually a compromise on uniform tariff legislation was reached by Congress—to the everlasting advantage of the country. James Madison's efforts concentrated on obtaining temporary tax laws to bolster the federal budget. Fitzsimmons favored permanent legislation. The list of dutiable articles proposed by Fitzsimmons covered a wide range of goods including beer and ale, beef, port, butter, candles, cordage, twine or packet thread, malt, nails, salt, tobacco, snuff, blankbooks, writing and printing materials, wrapping paper, leather, coaches and other four-wheeled carriages, nutmeg, cinnamon, cloves, figs, currants, almonds, and so on.

Congress agreed to the articles mentioned by Fitzsimmons, adding them to those on the Madison list. On April 11, 1789, legislation was devised for the permanent imposition of duties. While James Madison was considered the "father" of the legislation, Fitzsimmons was the force behind the framing of the bill.

Thirteen years after the signing of the Declaration of Independence at Philadelphia, on July 4, 1789, the first United States Tariff Act was signed into law in New York by George Washington. It became effective August 1. When Washington signed the Act, it included Madison's recommendations, those of Fitzsimmons, and many others offered by senators and representatives whose constituents resided in the mushrooming industrial centers of the North.

Except for the nomination of a chargé d'affaires at the Court of France on June 16, 1789, during the absence of Thomas Jefferson, the first presidential appointments ever made under the Constitution were Customs positions. On August 3, 1789, Washington sent to the Senate the nominations of fifty-nine collectors, thirty-three surveyors, and ten naval officers, the first presidential appointees in history. The list included heroes of the American Revolution who had fought with Washington, and his letters at that time leave no doubt that he considered these Revolutionary patriots the type of men needed to put the young republic on a solid financial and commercial foundation.

Gen. Benjamin Lincoln, who accepted the surrender of Cornwallis at Yorktown, became collector of Customs in Boston; Gen. Sharp Delaney became collector in Philadelphia; Gen. Otho Williams in Baltimore; and General John Lamb in New York, to name just a few. General Lamb was the hero of the capture of Fort Ticonderoga.

Further legislation in 1789 had created fifty-nine Customs districts in eleven states, under the supervision of collectors, "surveyors," and "naval officers." Every district was provided with a collector, but not every district was to have a "surveyor" or "naval officer." Not until the Tariff Act of 1922 was the designation of naval officer changed to Comptroller of Customs, but the functions of the job did not materially change from those listed in the Act of 1789.

The salaries for collectors consisted of the proceeds of specific fees and a commission on the sums paid to the Treasury. The commission was one-half of 1 percent at the larger ports and 1 percent at the others. Naval officers' salaries were based upon half of the fees collected, but without the commission. Surveyors, measurers, weighers, and gaugers were paid entirely from fees. This system remained in effect for many years.

The first political appointment by an American President was the appointment by George Washington of John Lamb to be the collector of Customs in New York.

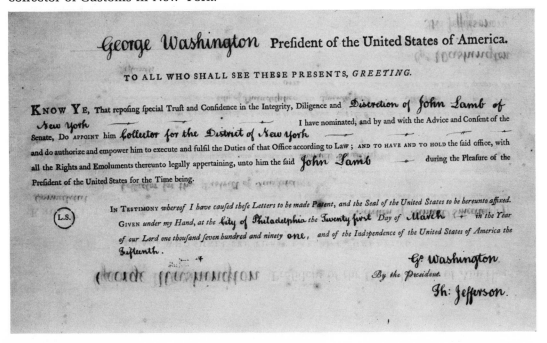

The Customhouse in Philadelphia as it
appeared in 1844.

All of this legislation was passed before the establishment of the Treasury
Department on September 2, 1789. Thus, U.S. Customs is a month older than the
department of which it is a part. The secretary of the treasury was ordered to
supervise the collection of federal revenue, and Customs officers were instructed
to keep their accounts in such manner as "may be directed by the proper department, or officers appointed by law to superintend the revenue of the United
States."

What is now the United States Public Health Service was for many years immediately under the jurisdiction of the collectors of Customs. An act of July 16,
1798, added to their duties the collection of hospital dues for the relief of sick and
disabled seamen, each foreign vessel being required to pay Customs collectors
twenty cents a month for every seaman employed. Collectors remained in charge
of the Marine Hospital Service, more as directors *ex officio*, until 1870, but they
continued to collect the fees on seamen until 1884.

For a long time the collectors, surveyors, and naval officers represented the
only federal presence in American cities and towns, save for judges, marshals,
and clerks of the courts. This inevitably led to the imposition on these Customs
officers of functions other than the collection of duties; often virtually any activity
having to do with shipping and navigation was assigned to Customs. Collectors
were appointed superintendents of lighthouses for certain districts under the
Lighthouse Act of August 7, 1789. An act passed in September of that same year,
governing the registry and clearing of vessels and the regulation of coastal trade,

placed the burden of the local administration of law on the Customs collectors, under general supervision of the secretary of the treasury.

The Customs Service had not yet reached its second birthday when the collectors received another assignment, this time as pension agents with the job of disbursing funds to discharged military personnel. Previously, each sovereign state had taken care of its own veterans. There was no mistaking the intent of the federal government in instituting this major policy shift. The troops now unequivocally belonged to the United States of America and not to its member states.

Nor was this the last of the unique responsibilities placed upon the collectors. The infant republic was in critical need of statistical data upon which to base its planning, its financial requirements, and its estimated tax needs. Alexander Hamilton's interest in productivity and industrial growth was expressed in a request made to collectors in 1791 asking that they transmit to the Treasury all documents which came into their possession relating to commerce, navigation, fisheries, or the manufactured products of the several states.

In 1809 the collectors were ordered to submit "all information in relation to the manufacturing establishments of the United States, and whatever suggestions that are calculated to foster and protect them." In 1829, they were asked to make "reports of the number and nature of persons engaged, and the kind and prices of salt manufactured." In 1831, they produced "statements regarding the quantity and quality of iron and steel in their forms"; in 1837, "reports on the propriety of establishing a system of telegraphs for the United States"; in 1845, "detailed statistics on the products of agriculture, mines and manufacture."

Thus was born the future Bureau of Census, which to this day continues to rely upon the United States Customs Service for data on a wide range of imported commodities, useful in providing economists with information for planning, for establishing regulatory quotas, making trade profiles, promoting tourism, and so on, all essential in estimating the balance of payments of the United States.

One year after Congress passed the first act for the regulation and collection of Customs duties in 1789, new legislation setting up machinery for the enforcement of the tariff laws, written mainly by Alexander Hamilton, passed Congress.

This remarkable piece of legislation provided the basis for many Customs regulations and practices that are still in effect. One section exempted from duty such sea stores on vessels and ships as were necessary for the subsistence of officers and crews while in port. Another paragraph exempted from duty all clothing, books, household furniture, and tools or implements of the trade or profession of persons arriving in the United States.

Other historic elements of the legislation provided for the "establishment, equipment, and maintenance of revenue cutters, or boats, not exceeding 10 in number." The act empowered collectors to employ small open rowboats and sailboats to be used by Customs officials in boarding ships and vessels. The cost was to be defrayed by the duties collected. Thus was born the United States Coast Guard, which was later to become an independent agency, part of the Treasury Department, and then in 1968 to be incorporated into the Department of

Transportation. To this day when Coast Guard officers are involved in a Customs enforcement action, they have the search-and-arrest power of Customs officers—a statutory authority that is not shared by any other arm of the executive branch of government, except the Immigration Service and the Drug Enforcement Administration.

One of the most significant sections of this legislation laid the foundation for the development of an interstate transportation system free from the imposition of local taxes or duties. The states had surrendered their right to impose and collect duty on goods passing from one member state to another. Although the language, stilted and somewhat obscure, does not appear in history books, this Act was an important historic document in that it helped to establish the sovereignty of the infant republic:

> So always and provided, that where goods, wares, or merchandise, of foreign growth or manufacture are to be transported to and from the respective ports of Philadelphia and Baltimore unto each other, through and across the State of Delaware, a manifest certified as aforesaid by the officers of that one of the said ports from whence the goods, wares, and merchandise, are to be so transported, shall be sufficient to warrant the transportation thereof to the other of the said ports without an immediate entry in the District of Delaware.

The provision was later amplified, authorizing the collector of the District of Pennsylvania to grant permits for the transportation of merchandise of foreign manufacture across the state of New Jersey to New York, or across the state of Delaware to any district in the states of Maryland or Virginia, and for the collector of New York to grant similar permits for the transportation of goods across the state of New Jersey, and for the collector of any district in Maryland or Virginia to grant permits for the transportation of goods across the states of Delaware to Pennsylvania.

Subsequent legislation decreed that all imported goods, wares, and merchandise would be dutiable based on actual costs at the "place of exportation," a regulation that is still on the books.

Until 1792, the principal officer in charge of Customs was an assistant to the secretary of the treasury. That office was abolished by the first session of the Second Congress, and a new job was created—the Commissioner of the Revenue, which was the antecedent of the present-day position of Commissioner of Internal Revenue. His original charter stated that he shall be responsible for "superintending, under the direction of the Head of the Department, the collection of the other revenue of the United States, and shall execute such other services, being comfortable to the Constitution." His annual salary was $1,900.

As finally approved, the tariff laws embraced a long list of specific duties, and five classes of goods taxed with *ad valorem* rates, that is, based on market values in the country of origin. They made provision for the refunding of duties on imported raw materials that were used in manufacturing and processing in the United States, and then reexported. This is technically referred to as "drawback." The laws also adopted the principle of discrimination in favor of commodities imported in vessels built or owned by citizens of the United States.

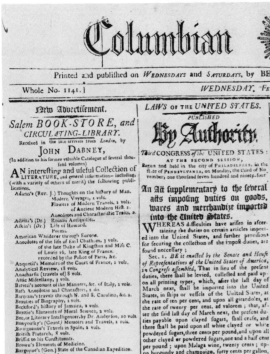

In 1795, at the second session of the Third Congress, meeting at Philadelphia, the customs duties on a wide range of imported commodities were modified and codified for the sake of clarity and to increase revenues. The law is here printed in a Boston newspaper of the time. Section four of the law deals with the well-known "drawback" procedure, whereby the importers of raw materials are entitled to a refund of their customs duties when finished manufactures are exported. This statute, which encouraged domestic industry, is still in effect.

Regarding specific duties, "spirits" were taxed up to ten cents per gallon; wines up to eighteen cents per gallon; beer, ale, and porter in casks, five cents per gallon; molasses two and one-half cents per gallon; tea from six to forty-five cents per pound; processed tobacco, six cents per pound; salt, six cents per bushel, and twine and packet thread two dollars per 112 pounds. Carriages and parts were

A record from 1790, kept by the collector of Customs, showing the quantity and value of a wide range of exports, as well as the countries that received them, for a little over a three-month period, from the port of Newport.

Return of Goods, Wares and Merchandize Exported from the District of Newport in the State of Rhode Island &c commencing the 21st of June and ending the 30th of September 1790

Species of Merchandize Exported	To England		Africa		French W. Indies		Nova Scotia		New Provid.		Florida		Total		Remarks
	Quantity	Value	Qy.	Value	Qy.	Value	Qy.	Value	Qy.	Value	Qy.	Value	Quantity	Value	
Apples					22 bbls	18.33					76	23.33	126 bbls	41.66	Produce of the United States
Ashes, Pot	3035	249											3035	249	Ditto Ditto
, Pearl	14.225	85.33											14.225	85.33	Ditto Ditto
Beef					13 tbs	104							13 bbl	104	Ditto Ditto
Boards, Pine			2000	12	62.500	417							74.500	429	Produce of United States
, Oak	4486	44.67											4486	44.67	Ditto Ditto
Butter					1820	177					150	729	9320	906	Ditto Ditto
Candles, Sperm: Cetl			6 boxes	66									6 boxes	66	Manufact: of United States
, Tallow			6 boxes	20									6 boxes	20	Ditto Ditto
Chaise & Sulkies					11	1100							11	1100	Manufacture of Ditto
Cheese					500 tb	31.25					2060	126	2560	156.25	Produce Ditto
Corn, Indian					330 tb	165.25	600	300	250	125			1180	590.25	Ditto Ditto
Fish, pickled											20	60	2235	7385	Fishery of United States
, dried					318	1756					9	15	887	1774	Ditto Ditto
, Salmon			6 half	24	10 bbl	80							15 bbl	104	Fishery foreign
Flour			24 bbl	168	510	3670							534 bbl	3738	Produce of the United States
Heading, Hogshead	5200	104											5200	104	Ditto Ditto
Hoops					10.500	225							20.560	225	Ditto Ditto
Hogs					104	340							104	340	Ditto Ditto
Horses					94	3760							94	3760	Ditto Ditto
Indigo	1 keg	12											1 keg	12	Ditto Ditto
Iron, Ship knees	87	29											87	29	Produce of United States
Lard					17 firk	85							17 firk	85	Ditto Ditto
Meal, Indian					158	230							158	230	Ditto Ditto
Oil, Whale					76	506.67							76	506.67	Ditto Ditto
Onions			1600	66.66	65.450	2727					500	20.84	67.550	2814.50	Ditto Ditto
Oxen					4	80							4 oxen	80	Ditto Ditto
Pitch	135	303.76											135 bbl	303.76	Ditto Ditto
Plank, White Oak	593	18											593	18	Ditto Ditto
Pork					69	690							69	690	Ditto Ditto
Potatoes					66	16.50	10	2.50			80	20	156	39	Ditto Ditto
Poultry					400	100							400	400	Ditto Ditto
Rice	6	75			76	1140							81	1215	Ditto Ditto
Rye							600	33.37					600	33.37	
Rum			43.431	14.477									43.431	14.477	Manufacd of United States
Shingles					20.000	60							20 mills	60	Ditto Ditto
Spirits of Turpentine	2	37.33											2 casks	37.33	Ditto Ditto
Staves, Barrel	2600	23.40			3000	27							5600	50.40	Produce of United States
, Butt	130	2.10											130	2.10	Ditto Ditto
, Hogshead	54.000	864			5000	80							59.000	944	Ditto Ditto
, Pipe					3872	62							3872	62	Ditto Ditto
Tarr	399	598.50											399	598.50	Ditto Ditto
Turpentine	68	226.66											68	226.66	Ditto Ditto
Tobacco	11 bbl	458.66	4 bbl	124.82	25	1000							40 bbl	1583.48	Ditto Ditto
Wax, Bees Wax	1 keg	20											1 keg	20	Ditto Ditto
Wool, Cotton					3 bags	133.66							3 bags	133.66	Foreign Produce
Saddles					23	53.66							23	53.66	Manufac: United States
Soap			6 boxes	20									6 boxes	20	Ditto Ditto
Sheep					235	235							235	235	Produce Ditto
		3351.41		14978.68		26221.32		335.87		125		996.17		46006.25	

Collectors Office District of Newport Oct 1st 1790
W. Ellery, Collector

As this 1790 Customs document shows,
some importers were allowed a substantial
discount for prompt payment of duties.

An Account of Discounts of 10 P. Cent. P. Annum, allowed sundry Persons for prompt payment of Duties, arising on Merchandize imported into the District of Newport commencing

When Entered	By whom	Vessels name	Masters name	From whence		Amount of Duty payable		Sum on which discount is allowed			Amount of Discount	
						dollars	Cts	dollars	Cts		doll	Cents
1790 July 20	Thomas Dennis	Good Intent	Thomas Dennis	Cape Francois	1	291	..	241	..	4 Mo.	8	.. 3
" " 21	Josiah Luther	Nancy	Josiah Luther	St. Eustatius	2	128	77	78	77	4 Mo.	2	.. 60
" " 26	Charles Wheaton	Abigail	Charles Wheaton	Aux cayes	3	220	67	170	67	4 Mo.	5	.. 68
" " 29	Peleg Wood	Industry	Peleg Wood	Port au Prince	4	113	18	63	18	4 Mo.	2	.. 10
" August 2	Caleb Gardner	Betsey	Wm. DWolf	St. Martins	5	202	1	152	1	4 Mo.	5	.. 6
" " 14	Barney Hicks	Polly	Barney Hicks	Cape Francis	6	63	70	13	70	4 Mo.	.	45
" " 21	Caleb Gardner	Hope	John Stanton	Havannah	7	198	86	158	86	4 Mo.	4	.. 96
" " 25	Lawrence & Lyon	Favorite	Isaac Lawrence	Cape Francis	8	130	23	80	23	4 Mo.	2	.. 67
			Collectors Office District of Newport October 1st 1790							Doll.	31	.. 55

assessed with an *ad valorem* duty of 15 percent, while goods not carried in American ships were subject to a 12½ percent tax. Tea was excluded from this restriction. On the free list were tin plates, wire, dyes, and furs.

The Neutrality Act

The outbreak of war between Great Britain and France in 1793 had triggered a series of aggressive acts against the transatlantic commerce of the United States, creating the necessity for new powers for the Customs collectors in order to control exports in addition to imports.

The United States government found itself at odds with both belligerent nations, which it charged with the violation of international law on four counts. The first complaint was that American vessels hauling breadgrain, the principal export of the United States, were not to be seized as vessels carrying "contraband of war." The second objection was that after notice of a port blockade, vessels en route to that port might be taken anywhere on the high seas. The United States held that the notice had no validity unless there was an actual blockading force outside the port. The third was the "Rule of 1756," under which the United States

SIR,

BY an inſtruction from this department, dated the 30th of May, 1793, the Collectors were informed that the *entry of veſſels captured and brought into our ports by the ſhips of war and privateers of France, and of their cargoes, was to be received in the ſame manner, under the ſame regulations and upon the ſame conditions, as the entry of veſſels which were not prizes; but that this privilege was not to extend to the belligerent powers at war with France, being contrary to the* 17th *and* 22d *articles of our treaty with that nation.*"

The *entry* and *ſale* in our ports, of prizes to privateers commiſſioned by France, not being ſtipulated in our treaty as a right, to be enjoyed by that nation, and there being an expreſs ſtipulation in the twenty-fourth article of the late treaty with Great-Britain, " that it ſhall not be lawful for any foreign privateers (not being ſubjects or citizens of " either of the ſaid parties) who have commiſſions from any other Prince or State in " enmity with either nation, to arm their ſhips in the ports of either of the ſaid parties, " or to ſell what they have taken, nor in any other manner to exchange the ſame." It has become neceſſary to vary the former inſtructions accordingly.

You will therefore obſerve that hereafter veſſels and property captured from the ſubjects of Great-Britain by privateers commiſſioned againſt that nation, are not to be admitted to an entry in the ports of the United States; of courſe any goods or property landed therefrom will be ſubject to ſeizure as being imported contrary to law.

The Collectors will recollect that the ſecurity of the Revenue and the faith of the United States, are highly concerned in preventing the introduction for conſumption and ſale of any goods or property by prizes to privateers; when ſuch veſſels appear in our ports, they will therefore cauſe extraordinary care and vigilance to be obſerved.

The 22d article of our treaty with France and the 24th article of our treaty with Great-Britain contain ſtipulations *that privateers* commiſſioned againſt either of the parties ſhall not be allowed to purchaſe *more proviſions than ſhall be neceſſary to their going to the neareſt port of that Prince or State from whom they obtained commiſſions;* if therefore the privateers of either nation exceed what is permitted in this reſpect, immediate reports are to be made to the Governor of the State, and Attorney of the Diſtrict.

I am with Conſideration
Sir your Obed Servant
Oliver Wolcott

William Webb Esq
Collector Bath

A memorandum to Customs collectors, circulated just one year before the French Revolution, dealing with the problem of excluding from the United States goods seized by English and French privateers.

denied the right of Great Britain to interfere in her trade with the French and Spanish colonies. The fourth was the assertion that "free ships make free goods," that a neutral vessel was not subject to capture, no matter whose property it carried.

To prevent the capture of American ships, Congress ordered them to remain at domestic ports and stay off the high seas, an action that was repeated before the War of 1812. A series of emergency decrees were adopted. They included a joint resolution placing a thirty-day embargo on all vessels in U.S. ports, directing that no customs clearance be given except on specific orders of the President. Furthermore, vessels were not permitted to trade between U.S. ports without a bond filed with the collectors, certifying that the cargo would be delivered in the United States. The export of munitions was banned for one year. Penalties were imposed for the repair and outfitting of ships to be employed in hostile acts against countries with which the United States was at peace.

Customs collectors were charged with enforcing these laws, which were lumped together under the Neutrality Act. To this day this is still a Customs function.

In June 1798, commercial relations with France were cut off by Congress, and collectors were instructed to refuse clearance to ships bound for a foreign country unless the masters posted bond certifying they would not trade with France or a French colony. Public opinion against the belligerents was aroused to such an extent that Congress adopted the Alien and Sedition Acts requiring aliens to register with a clerk of the court or a Customs collector. Shipmasters were required to report the names of arriving aliens to collectors for transmittal to the Department of State. The President was empowered to order the expulsion of any alien deemed to be "dangerous to the peace and the safety of the country."

Weights and Measures

The beginnings of the development of weights and measures go back to prehistoric times. Units of length were derived from the limbs of the human body. They included the length of the foot, the width of the palm, and the length of the forearm. The inch was originally gauged by the thumb. Eventually more exact measurements were fixed and standardized.

One of the earliest units, the foot, was the length of the ordinary human limb. Then the length of the foot of various tribal rulers became the standard of measurement, but there was of course no uniformity. The foot was used successively by the Egyptians, the Greeks, and the Romans. The concept was absorbed by Britain from the Romans, and it was finally defined in Great Britain as one-third of the British Imperial Yard.

The early pioneers brought with them the weights and measures in use in their homelands, enabling them to carry on commercial relations. As settlements grew and different customs and usages were introduced, a strong need for standardization developed. Colonial leaders had provided for this omission in the Articles of Confederation: "The United States in Congress assembled shall also have sole and exclusive right and power of fixing the standards of weights and measures throughout the United States." The Continental Congress appointed a committee in 1783, consisting of Alexander Hamilton, the delegate from New York, and James Madison, of Virginia, to formulate regulations for units and systems of weights and measure. George Washington, in a message to his Secretary of State Thomas Jefferson, said in 1790: "Uniformity in the currency, weights, and measure of the United States is an object of great importance, and will, I am persuaded, be duly attended to."

By historic coincidence, both the French and British were debating concurrently uniformity in weights and measures. Jefferson joined the statesmen of these countries in the hope that a universal system could be adopted. However, as the issue became more confused with each passing year, the legislators were happy to acquiesce in the standards accepted by the individual states of the Union. Congressional committee after committee met and submitted reports. In 1796 the House of Representatives formed itself into a Committee of the Whole to consider Jefferson's recommendations. Experiments with weights and measures were carried out in Philadelphia but no standards were found to be acceptable.

In 1799, Congress ordered the surveyor of each Customs port of the United States "from time to time, and particularly on the first Monday of January and July in each year," to examine and try the weights and measures in use, along with other instruments used in ascertaining customs duties on imports. It directed that standards be provided for each Customs collector at public expense. When disagreements and errors were discovered, the surveyors were to report them to the collectors with a request that they make adjustments in accordance with Treasury Department standards.

Although this was actually the first Weights and Measures Act passed by Congress, because no uniform standards had been agreed upon, the legislation was not effective for many years.

In 1813 a brass bar was made by Troughton of London for the Coast Survey, then part of the Treasury Department, and brought to the United States by Coast Survey Superintendent Ferdinand R. Hassler and adopted as the standard length, a yard of thirty-six inches. This was a step in the right direction.

In his 1816 message to Congress, President Madison deplored the fact that no provision had been made for the uniformity of weights and measures, and he suggested that they begin by adopting the decimal system proposed by Thomas Jefferson. In 1821 the Speaker placed before the House of Representatives a report by Secretary of State John Quincy Adams, an elaborate and well-docu-

Some early standard measures in use during the nineteenth century—two bronze one-gallon pitchers, a half-bushel measure, and a hydrometer used to test imported whiskey.

mented in-depth study of the vastly complex subject, on the basis of which the Mint Act of 1828 was passed.

This act based American standards of weight on the British parliamentary pound. This was the first legislation to produce results in the establishment of uniform weights. An exact replica of the British parliamentary or Imperial brass pound, as it is commonly known, was fashioned with meticulous care. It was procured by Albert Gallatin, United States Minister to London and was sent to the Director of the Mint at Philadelphia by special messenger. The importance of the occasion was reflected in the ceremony surrounding it. The replica remained untouched until President Adams made a trip to Philadelphia to verify Gallatin's seal and the authenticity of the transaction.

Congress had also directed the secretary of the treasury to make a comparison of the standards of weights and measures in use at the principal customhouses in the United States and report his findings to the Senate. This responsibility also fell upon the shoulders of Superintendent Ferdinand R. Hassler. His report showed that some large discrepancies did exist, but the average value of the various units agreed fairly well with the weights and measures in use in Great Britain at the time of the American Revolution. Secretary of the Treasury McLane stated:

> This is nevertheless a serious evil, inasmuch as it produces inequalities in the duties levied at the different ports; and thus contravenes the spirit of the Constitution which declares that all duties, imposts, and excises shall be uniform throughout the United States. It is believed however, that this department has full authority to correct the evil, by causing uniform and accurate weights and measures, and authentic standards, to be supplied to all custom houses.

With this authority, the secretary instructed Mr. Hassler to proceed with the construction of weights and measures. Before this could be done it was necessary to select the units and prepare the standards. The Office of Standard Weights and Measures of the Treasury decided upon the avoirdupois pound of 7,000 grains (derived from the Mint), the gallon of 231 cubic inches, and the Winchester bushel of 2,150.42 cubic inches.

Construction of the weights and measures began in earnest. While Hassler and his associates were working with feverish haste to complete the task, a request was sent to Congress to try again to establish a science of measurement. Congress, by resolution, directed the secretary of the treasury to cause a complete set of all weights and measures, the same as those in process of manufacture for use in the several customhouses, to be adopted as standards and delivered to the governors of each state of the Union "to the end that a uniform standard of weights and measures may be established throughout the United States." The Office of Weights and Measures was transferred from the Treasury to the newly created National Bureau of Standards in 1901.

The Customs Ensign

The Customs flag, almost as familiar at ports of entry as Old Glory itself, was first authorized by Congress on March 2, 1799, for Hamilton's new Revenue Cutter

The unique design of the Customs ensign
here contrasts with a more familiar design
as both flags fly atop Customs headquarters
in Washington.

Service. The flag is known officially as the Customs ensign or the revenue ensign.

Two years after the flag of the United States was adopted, Congress provided "that the cutters and boats employed in the service of the revenue shall be distinguished from other vessels by an ensign and pennant, with such marks thereon as shall be prescribed and directed by the President of the United States . . ."

On August 1, 1799, Oliver Wolcott, second secretary of the treasury, issued an order on authority of the President that the ensign and pennant should consist of "16 perpendicular stripes, alternate red and white, the union of the ensign to be the arms of the United States in dark blue on a white field."

There is little statutory evidence to substantiate the legend, but the tradition that grew with and became part of the U.S. Customs story implies that the flag was built around historic symbols. The sixteen vertical stripes in the body are said to represent the original thirteen states, plus Vermont, Kentucky, and Tennessee, which had joined the Union by the time the Customs ensign was officially adopted.

In the union of the flag are the eagle, the national emblem of the United States, thirteen stars, thirteen leaves in the olive branch, thirteen arrows, and thirteen bars to the shield, all corresponding to the number of states constituting the Union at the time of the founding of the republic.

Although the Customs ensign was originally intended to be flown only on revenue cutters and boats performing Customs service, the practice of unfurling it atop customhouses grew until it became traditional. It wasn't until 1874 that Secretary of the Treasury William A. Richardson directed the flag to be flown from all customhouses across the nation. From that time until 1910, the revenue pennant was displayed universally on customhouses, Customs boats, and revenue cutters.

When the Coast Guard became an arm of the Treasury Department and the duties of the Revenue Cutter Service were removed from Customs, a change in the flag became necessary. Because the particular ensign, the sign of authority of a Coast Guard vessel, was authorized for no purpose other than the one originally contemplated by Congress, President William Howard Taft issued an Executive Order on June 7, 1910, announcing that "the flag now used by vessels of the Revenue Cutter Service be marked by the distinctive emblem of that Service, in blue and white, placed on a line with the lower edge of the union, and over the center of the seventh vertical red stripe . . ."

Today the banner of the United States Customs Service remains the original ensign authorized by Congress in 1799. In compliance with a presidential order in 1962, the ensign flies twenty-four hours a day at every U.S. port of entry.

An early newspaper illustration showing Customs inspectors at work at New York's piers.

Which section of the Tariff Act would cover Sophia Loren? Actually, the figure in the box is wax and depicts the Academy Award-winning actress in a scene from the film *Two Women*. It was imported for a Hollywood wax museum.

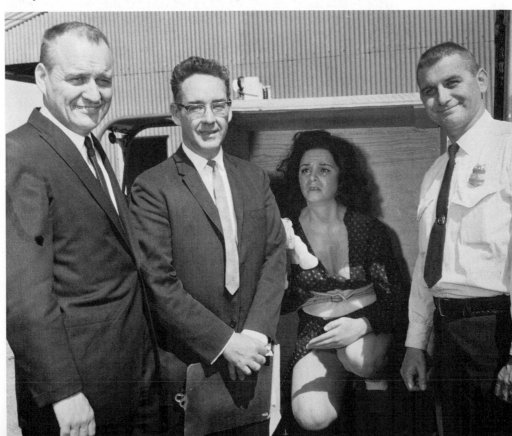

chapter four

The Evolving Customs Laws

The import laws of the United States are legion and they are a barometer of the economic and political conditions prevailing at the time of their enactment. In the years between 1800 and 1890, Congress passed 260 acts affecting or amending the tariff laws of America. They have been endlessly analyzed by countless writers of various schools of economic persuasion, the "high protectionists," the "medium protectionists," the "low tariff" advocates, and the exponents of the doctrine of free trade.

Wars invariably heighten the need of the belligerent powers for additional revenue, and so taxes go up. In peacetime, as industrialization takes hold in economically emerging nations, tariff barriers are built to protect new industries. Quotas are imposed on imports by one nation, whether of raw materials or manufactured goods, in retaliation for restrictions placed on that nation's exports. And so it goes.

The tariff laws are, in the words of former Commissioner of Customs Philip Nichols, Jr., an "intractable mass of material," consisting of two centuries of "received wisdom," a huge and never-ending effort to provide for the Customs officer a rule for every possible situation that might be encountered in the performance of duties. Some of these statutes are so carefully and delicately worded that the slightest error or misinterpretation could cost the Treasury large sums. Even an error in punctuation, or a misreading of the text, could prove costly, as demonstrated by the classic *comma case*, celebrated in Customs history.

A clerk changed the punctuation in the language of the free list of the Tariff Act of 1872, inserting a comma instead of a hyphen. The provision then read: "Tropical fruit, plants, etc." It should have read: "Tropical fruit-plants, etc." As a result, all tropical fruit entered the United States free of duty, although Congress had intended that only tropical fruit-plants were to enjoy this privilege.

Duties on tropical fruits were collected by Customs officers according to the intent of Congress, but importers protested all the collections, basing their case on the letter of the law. When the case reached the Supreme Court, the Justices were compelled to decide in favor of the importers, and the country was deprived of $3 million in revenue before Congress could correct the language in another legislative act two years later.

Duties are generally defined as taxes on goods, wares, and merchandise imported or exported. Customs duties are either "specific" or *ad valorem*. A "specific" duty is one based on or reckoned by the quantity of goods imported, by weight, measure, or number; *ad valorem* duty is based on the value of the imported goods; that is, the cost of the merchandise in the country of origin. A widespread and perennial complaint that specific duties protect from foreign competition only the lower grades of goods forced a careful breakdown of the *ad valorem* rates.

Other more complicated formulas are often employed—as where an article is classified according to its value and receives a different *ad valorem* rate in each category of merchandise, or again when classified according to specific characteristics and taxed at different *ad valorem* rates, though these combinations are classed as *ad valorem* rates. America's Tariff Act of 1907 demonstrates the tremendous complications of a tariff law. Here, out of 444 paragraphs, 246 deal with specific rates, 106 with *ad valorem*, and 92 with mixed rates.

Proper "liquidation," a technical term referring to the final determination of the amount of a specific duty, is much simpler than the liquidation of an *ad valorem* or mixed rate. The statements of value made under oath by importers or consignees are not always considered absolute and final by appraising officers, and so liquidation often involves a second review of duties imposed after merchandise has entered the country.

The Treasury Department, through administrative regulation and Congressional enactment, has built up a complex system for ascertaining the true *ad valorem* value of dutiable goods, and additional safeguards are being provided all the time. The greater the number of goods subject to *ad valorem* duties, the more complicated becomes the work of the people who appraise the merchandise.

The tariff acts from 1789 to 1816 show marked increases in duties and the addition of many items to the *ad valorem* class, often transferred there from the specific category. Many new items were given mixed rates as well.

On July 1, 1812, Congress passed a supplemental tariff act increasing by 100 percent the existing duties on imported goods. It was to take effect immediately and continue during the war with Great Britain and until the expiration of one year after the peace treaty. On February 5, 1816, the operations of the law were extended to June 30 of that same year, with a proviso that from then until a new list of duties was established, the rate of increase would be 42 instead of 100 percent as established by the 1812 Act.

Though slavery existed until the Civil War, the slave trade itself had been circumscribed by an Act of Congress in 1807 prohibiting the importation of slaves from foreign countries. This Customs manifest of 1849, dealing with the transport of slaves from New Orleans to Galveston, certifies that the slaves were in fact brought from New Orleans and not some foreign port.

There were many reasons for these increases. The United States had experienced serious troubles with Great Britain, France, and the powers of the Barbary coast—Algiers, Tunis, Tripoli, and Morocco. Wars cost money and there is always a big drop in customs revenue because of the absence of imports from belligerent nations.

A series of embargoes and nonintercourse acts were enacted by the United States, aimed at Great Britain. In the early nineteenth century, the Barbary powers were pirates on the high seas, to the great detriment of the United States, capturing seamen, merchandise, vessels, and anything they could lay their hands on.

An act passed on March 26, 1804, provided for the building, arming, and equipping of two sixteen-gun men-of-war for service in the Mediterranean against the Regency of Tripoli. An additional duty of 2½ percent was levied on goods taxed at *ad valorem* rates. An additional 10 percent duty was ordered on all goods

SALEM GAZETTE.

VOLUME XXVII.] SALEM, (MASSACHUSETTS,) TUESDAY, DECEMBER 21, 1813. No. 102.

OF GENERAL MOREAU.

From the Boston Daily Advertiser.

THE writer of this paſſed an evening in London in 1804, with our late miniſter to France Joel Barlow, and the converſation turned upon the recent murder of the Duke D'Enghien, by order of Bonaparte. Of this atrocious deed, Mr Barlow expreſſed the moſt unqualified deteſtation and horror, and mentioned ſome incidents not generally known relating to that event.

General Moreau had recently been tried and baniſhed from his native country, and knowing that Mr. Barlow's ſources of information was favorable to a correct knowledge of the crime alledged and the views of the Tyrant in bringing him to trial—I aſked him what was the public ſentiment upon the occaſion. He anſwered—Moreau's life was to have been ſacrificed as was D'Enghien, but the power of the Emperor could not effect his meditated deſtruction—Moreau was the idol of the people, and when it was known that his life was in danger, and his trial pending, an immenſe concourſe of people aſſembled in front of the hall where his accuſers were ſitting—the ſymptoms of commotion were ſo violent that *thrice* did the Judges, as Mr. Barlow declared, ſend to the Emperor that unleſs they were permitted to acquit Moreau there would be an inſurrection—twice, ſaid Barlow, did Bonaparte ſend them his *mandate to condemn this innocent man*, but the third time yielded to the fear of the inevitable conſequences, and permitted them to ſpare his life. A friend who was preſent at this intereſting criſis in the hiſtory of Moreau, has aſſured me that a park of artillery ſurrounded the hall of juſtice, ready loaded and the matches were lighted to play upon the people if any attempt to reſcue the General was made during this trial, which ended at midnight, when twenty-thouſand men ſtood ready to ſacrifice their lives the moment the ſentence of condemnation was paſſed. This is the traitor to his country and king, as this celebrated General is now ſtyled by the wretches who triumph in his fall.—Oh! my countrymen, if we can ſympathiſe with thoſe who rejoice in the termination of this Hero's life, we are deſerving of the chains of his vindictive perſecutor, the "Superemiment Napoleon."

General Moreau's Death.

FROM LONDON PAPERS.

General MOREAU to Madam MOREAU.

My Dear Love—At the battle of Dreſden, three days ago, I had my two legs carried off by a cannon ball.

That ſcoundrel Bonaparte is always fortunate.

The amputation was performed as well as poſſible.

Though the army has made a retrograde movement, it is not at all the conſequence of defeat, but from a want of enſemble, and in order to get nearer Gen. Blucher.

Excuſe my haſty writing I love and embrace you with all my heart.

Rapatel will finiſh. V. M.

Madame—The General permits me to write to you on the ſame ſheet on which he has ſent you a few lines. Judge of my grief and regret by what he has juſt told you.

From the moment he was wounded, I have not left him, nor will I leave him till he is perfectly cured. We have the greateſt hopes, and I who know him, am certain we ſhall ſave him. He ſupported the amputation with heroic courage, without fainting. The firſt dreſſing has been taken off and the wounds have a good appearance He had only a ſlight acceſs of fever when the ſuppuration took place, and it has conſiderably diminiſhed.

Forgive theſe details; they are as painful to me to give as they will be to you to receive. I have ſtood in need of all my fortitude for the laſt four days, and ſhall ſtill ſtand in need of it. Rely upon my care, my friendſhip, and upon all the ſentiments with which both of you have inſpired me; don't alarm yourſelf—I need not tell you to exert your courage. I know your heart.

I will neglect no opportunity to write to you—The Surgeon has juſt aſſured me that if he continues to go on as well, he will be well enough in five weeks to go out in a carriage.

Madame and reſpectable friend, farewell—I am miſerable. Kiſs poor Iſabelle for your moſt devoted ſervant, RAPATEL.

Lunn, [illegible] 30. 1813.

Sept. 1—He is going on well, and is eaſy.

Extract of a letter from Toplitz, Sept. 4

"POOR MOREAU died yeſterday He was in the act of giving ſome [illegible]pinion on military matters, while paſſing with the Emperor of Ruſſia behind a Pruſſian battery, to which two French batteries were anſwering, one in front and the other in flank, and Lord Cathcart and Sir R. Wilſon were liſtening to him, when a cannon ball ſtruck his thigh and almoſt carried his leg off, paſſed through his horſe, and ſhattered his other leg to pieces. He gave a deep groan at firſt, but immediately after the firſt agony of pain was over, he called for a ſegar. They bore him off the field on a litter made of Coſſack's pikes, and carried him to a cottage at a ſhort diſtance, which, however, was ſo much expoſed to the fire, that they were obliged, after juſt binding up his wounds, to remove him further off to the Emperor's quarters, where one leg was amputated, he ſmoking the whole time. When the ſurgeon informed him that he muſt deprive him of his other, he obſerved, without ſhewing any pain or peeviſhneſs, but in the calmeſt manner, that had he known that before his other was cut off, he ſhould have preferred dying The litter on which they had hitherto conveyed him was covered with nothing but wet ſtraw, and a cloak drenched through with rain, which continued in torrents the whole day.—They now placed more cloaks over him, and laid him more comfortably on a good litter, in which he was carried to Dippoldeſwalde; but long before his arrival there, he was ſoaked through and through. He was brought however ſafely to Lunn, where he ſeemed to be going on well, till a long conference, which took place between him and three or four of the allied Generals, by which he was completely exhauſted. Soon after this he became extremely ſick, and hourly grew worſe. Through the whole of his ſufferings he bore his fate with a heroiſm and grandeur of mind not to be ſurpaſſed, and appeared to thoſe with whom he converſed to endure but little pain, from his extreme compoſure and calmneſs. He died at 8 o'clock yeſterday morning."

Madame Moreau—As ſoon as the account reached this country of the death of the gallant Moreau, the Prince Regent expreſſed a wiſh to pay a viſit of condolence to his afflicted widow: but ſhe was in ſtrong convulſions. Theſe continued for ſome days, and were ſucceeded by a calm more afflicting, perhaps, than thoſe burſts of tears and ſorrow which give relief to the overcharged heart.

The following Letter was written by the Emperor Alexander to Madame Moreau, upon the demiſe of her huſband.

"MADAM—When the dreadful misfortune which befel Gen Moreau, cloſe to my ſide, deprived me of the talents and experience of that great man, I indulged the hope, that, by care, we might ſtill be able to preſerve him to his family and to my friendſhip. PROVIDENCE has ordered it otherwiſe. He died as he lived, in the full vigor of a ſtrong and ſteady mind. There is but one remedy for the great miſeries of life—that of ſeeing them participated. In Ruſſia, Madam, you will find theſe ſentiments every where; and if it ſuit you to fix your reſidence there, I will do all in my power to embelliſh the exiſtence of a perſonage of whom I make it my ſacred duty to be the conſoler and the ſupport.

I entreat you, Madam, to rely upon it irrevocably: never let me be in ignorance of any circumſtance in which I can be of any uſe to you, and write directly to me always To anticipate your wiſhes will be a pleaſure to me The friendſhip I vowed to your huſband exiſts beyond the grave, and I have no other means of ſhewing it, at leaſt in part, towards him, than by doing every thing in my power to enſure the welfare of his family.—In theſe ſad and cruel circumſtances, accept, Madam, theſe marks of friendſhip, and the aſſurance of all my ſentiments.

"ALEXANDER."

"Toplitz, 6th Sept. 1813."

POLITICAL MISCELLANY.

From the CENTINEL.

THE ROAD TO RUIN.—No. VI.

ON THE EFFECTS OF THIS UNJUST WAR ON THE MERCHANTS.

* * * * SPECULATION is the inevitable fruit of a fluctuating market. Mercantile men will perfectly underſtand me when I ſay that there is a *melancholy* pleaſure in making money on foundations ſo very inſecure; and that one dollar, fairly gained in ſafe and ſecure times, is worth five obtained in times ſo pregnant with anxiety and danger.

The preſent ſpeculations rather reſemble the hazards of a gaming table, in which the chance of the *die*, rather than the agreeable, honorable exerciſe of mercantile ſagacity and foreſight, direct thhe operations and quicken the exertions of the induſtrious merchant.

I may hazard one more abſtract remark, which will be perfectly intelligible, and univerſally admitted by merchants: That commerce is in a dangerous, unprofitable and unnatural ſtate, when the adventurer is obliged to calculate all the riſksof *political* events; when he cannot truſt his bread upon the waters with ſecurity without taking into the account the follies, caprice, errors and wickedneſs of ſtateſmen; when he knows not whether peace, unexpectedly accepted, may not defeat his ſchemes;—whether Embargo may not blaſt his foreign adventures, or, by its deleterious effects on the people, double the value of the articles on hand—or whether a protracted, inexorable, ruinous War, is deſtined to raiſe all the articles of foreign growth to an immoderate, and, to the people ruinous price. * * * *

I now come to more *practical* remarks—*Here* you will find a merchant hugging himſelf in the ſuppoſed profits which he has made by the ſale of a large cargo of coffee at thirty-three or thirty-four cents, which coſt him but ſixteen. This is mighty well! and very natural—and if he has made his fortune by this ſpeculation, he lays his money by in eagles or half eagles, it is perhaps ſecure—unleſs the Britiſh ſhould, in retaliation for Mr. Madiſon's inhumanity, in butchering *her ſubjects* becauſe ſhe puniſhes her *traitors*, lay our cities in aſhes—and ſeize his eagles.

But moſt men, exhilarated by theſe unnatural profits, will be ſtimulated, like gamblers, to go on—and try their fortunes again.

PEACE muſt finally come; and it may come like the WAR, as *a thief and robber* in the night;—and it may find him with one hundred thouſand dollars worth of ſugar at twenty-five or twenty-ſeven dollars, or of indigo at five or ſeven dollars It may fall fifty or more per cent—and his imagined fortune will vaniſh at a ſtroke.

This is no fanciful picture—Every man flatters himſelf that *he* has ſagacity to eſcape. But it is certain that when PEACE does come, (and come it muſt) when the people, who are the victims and ſufferers from their high prices and ruinous taxes ſhall awake, many muſt and will be *caught and ruined.*

Conſidered, therefore, as a great claſs of the community, the merchants probably will be great loſers in the end by this diſaſtrous War. It may be laid down as a certain axiom, that PEACE is the *patroneſs* of commerce, and WAR its *perſecutrix.*

Again,—It ſhould be conſidered, that if merchants make in ſome few inſtances large profits, at the expence of the *poor*, the mechanic, the widow, the orphan, the ſalaryman, and the farmer, a *large* ſhare of this profit goes to foreign ſeamen and foreign merchants, who are the freighters of the goods introduced; all of which was before ſhared among ourſelves—Nor is this all—theſe foreigners having taſted the profits of our trade, being brought from the Black Sea and the Baltic to know the immenſe trade opened in this country, they may contrive to ſupply the ſouthern States after the Peace, and thus, perhaps, the right-hand of Northern commerce may be amputated.

Another effect produced by the War on the mercantile part of ſociety, and extending its baneful operations and poiſonous influence through the whole body politic, is the deſtruction of mercantile honor and probity. In dangerous times the wiſe and prudent ſhrink from bold adventure. The temptation of exorbitant profit, calls into activity an indigent, reſtleſs, unprincipled claſs of men, who tremble at no dangers, and are ſtartled at no meaſures.

Encouraged and protected from infamy by the juſt odium againſt the War, they engage in lawleſs ſpeculations, ſneer at the reſtraints of conſcience, laugh at perjury, mock at legal reſtraints, and acquire an ill-gotten wealth at the expence of public morals—and of the more ſober, conſcientious part of the mercantile community. If theſe effects would be only co-exiſtent with the War; if one could ſafely expect a miraculous return to good principles with a diſtant, very diſtant Peace, we might have ſome conſolation. But this gangrene in the body politic will have taken too deep root to be extirpated by the lancet or the cautery. Adminiſtration hirelings may revile the Northern States, and the merchants generally, for this monſtrous depravation of morals—this execrable courſe of ſmuggling and fraud—but there is a *Juſt GOD*, who knows how to trace the cauſes of human events, and he will, aſſuredly, viſit upon the Authors of this War all the iniquities of which it has been the occaſion. If the guilty deſerve our ſcorn or our pity, the *tempters* and ſeducers deſerve our execration.

But there is a view in which this War will be contemplated by enlightened merchants and profound ſtateſmen, in which its effects on the commerce of this country will be ſeen to be moſt diſaſtrous, and for which our poſterity will have occaſion to execrate its authors, perhaps for ages. It may be conceded that a meaſure may be temporarily ruinous to the exiſting merchant, and yet productive of eventual national good. The caſe, indeed, is a rare one; and the politician ought to be extremely ſure of his calculation before he attempts ſo hazardous an experiment. But what ſhall we ſay to a meaſure ruinous in its immediate effects, and fatal to the permanent intereſts of a country?

Such a meaſure was this unneceſſary and unjuſt War.—The very Adminiſtration themſelves pretend that Britain was jealous of our commercial proſperity.—*Even ſome federaliſts*, in ſpite of that dignified forbearance with which Great-Britain had witneſſed a ſucceſſion of meaſures hoſtile to her, and p[illegible] and favorable to her enemy, entertained [illegible] ſame unfounded jealouſy of her views.

What ſhall we ſay then to a policy, which, believing in her ſyſtematic rivalſhip, invited her to pounce upon our defenceleſs commerce and to drive it from the ocean?

Where now is that canvas which whitened every ſea? Where that hardy induſtry, and bold adventure, which affronted peril, and vexed every ocean? Some fifty faſt ſailing ſchooners, ſkulking in and out of the ports of France, bringing us brandies to poiſon, and ribbons and feathers to decorate our miſery, and ſome hundred jebecque boats ſtealing in the night along our coaſts, make up the *grand* total of the commerce of ſeven millions of the hardieſt, boldeſt, moſt adventurous people, on earth. Theſe are the *bleſſings* of this War. Our foreign commerce inſured at fifty per cent; that of our enemies ſailing ſcarcely at five—We are teaching our enemy and all the world to live without us—and when a tardy Peace ſhall arrive; when Mr. Madiſon's War appetite ſhall have been ſatiated, we ſhall then ſee every port either ſhut to our commerce, or giving us a cold, unwelcome, unprofitable reception. In the mean time our enemy is exploring new ſcenes of adventure—is forming new ties and new connexions, and extending that ſucceſsful commerce ſo much the object of the hatred, the jealouſy and the enmity of Meſſrs. Madiſon, Bonaparte and Jefferſon. Should this War laſt ten years, it will take a century to regain the footing we have voluntarily ſacrificed in the trade of the world.—Shut out from India, excluded by the common policy of Europe from their colonies, with a reduced capital, an exorbitant debt, and diminiſhed ſeamen, we ſhall have to recommence a new conteſt with a rival who has been thriving at our expenſe.

GOV. SULLIVAN.

We recommend for the perusal of Democrats the following extract from the late Gov SULLIVAN's "*Obſervations upon the Government of the United States.*" His remarks are very pertinent to the ſubject of the Conqueſt of Canada, a diſorder of which the country is not yet cured

"THE ancient republics loſt their freedom by their pride of conqueſt; the pulſe of their nations beat high for military achievements; while our ambition ought not to be to conquer countries, but to render ourſelves, and other nations, happy.

The wiſe man ſaid truly, "Pride goeth before a fall." The ancient republics, by inſtituting triumphs, and exhibiting the calamities and miſeries of their fellow-men, as the means of the higheſt honors to themſelves, exterminated the proper feelings of humanity. Their pride for conqueſt rendered large armies neceſſary: The leaders of the armies conſidered themſelves as the moſt deſerving part of the community; and to wreſt from the public thoſe riches and honors which they thought to be the juſt reward of their ſkill and courage, they turned the ſwords of their legions againſt the freedom of their country, and deſtroyed it

But Americans ought to deſpiſe the laurels that are reaped from the miſeries of mankind Conqueſt will forever introduce, as it did in Greece and Italy, a thirſt for perſonal dominion, as well as inequality of riches and luxury. Theſe are quite incompatible with all ideas of civil liberty; and the *hope of conqueſt ought to be abhorred by every American.*"

JEFFERSON'S PUZZLE.

From the (Phila.) Daily Advertiser, Dec. 6.

Extract of a letter from THOMAS JEFFERSON, *to a gentleman in Pennſylvania, dated*

MONTICELLO, Oct. 3, 1813.

"No man on earth has a ſtronger deteſtation than myſelf of the unprincipled Tyrant who is deluging the Continent of Europe with blood—no one was more gratified by the diſaſters of the laſt Campaign, nor wiſhed more ſincerely ſucceſs to the efforts of the virtuous ALEXANDER."

From the Chronicle.

"We do not believe Mr. JEFFERSON ever wrote the above, or that it contains his ſentiments"

From the (Phil.) D. Advertiſer, Dec 12.

It having been intimated to the Editor, that doubts were entertained as to the authenticity of the foregoing extract, publiſhed on the 6th inſt. he thinks it due as well to his fellow-citizens, as to himſelf, to declare, that the letter, from which the extract was faithfully made, was really written by THOMAS JEFFERSON, late Preſident of the United States, and addreſſed by him to a reſpectable gentleman of this State, between whom and Mr Jefferſon there has been for many years, & ſtill is, a ſtrong perſonal attachment.

From the NEW-YORK GAZETTE.

We have ſeen a letter from a gentleman of this city, now at Philadelphia, who is intimate with Dr LOGAN He writes that the Doctor declared to him, that the letter from Thomas Jefferſon recently publiſhed in all the papers, was genuine; that the original was in his poſſeſſion, and that any perſon was welcome to ſee it—Will the Democratic editors *ſtill* deny it? Yes! Will they not do any thing to ſerve their own purpoſes?

A Salem newspaper of 1813. With the Napoleonic Wars raging in Europe, and America at war with Britain, trade with both allies and belligerents was severely restricted. The editorial beginning at the bottom of the second column complains about these trade restrictions and suggests that Britain is our traditional ally and that the war with her is unnecessary.

SALEM GAZETTE.

Volume XXVII.]   SALEM, (Massachusetts,) FRIDAY, December 31, 1813.   [No. 105.

MISCELLANY.

From the Boston Daily Advertiser.

The strong features of the Disfranchifing Act, improperly called by the more fafcinating name of Embargo.

MY FELLOW CITIZENS,

I congratulate you. The meafure of your wrongs and fufferings is full. It is not in the power of malicious ingenuity to devife new torments. You now know the worft, and you have only to fummon all your fortitude and philofophy to endure this act and you will merit the character of heroes and the crown of faints.—Patience under affliction is one of the firft of human virtues, and fubmiffion under accumulated wrongs is certainly the very firft in the character of a good French or American citizen. If this act had never been made, your loyalty never could have been put to the fevereft teft. It might have remained uncertain whether you were capable of bearing more than ever men bore. Even Mr. Madifon, or Judge Story, or Mr. Gray, or Ben. Auftin will give you the praife of forbearance and meeknefs, if you kifs this fcorpion rod.— I have heard you cenfured for the imitation of the character of Job. They do you injuftice. You are no more refponfible for this (what fome perfons call) bafe fubmiffive fpirit, than one of the Britifh officers in a ftone prifon under three iron doors

commemoration of the landing of our brave Forefathers, when they fled from perfecution to this *land of freedom,* I hope Judge Story will be appointed to deliver the difcourfe.

The fubject ought to be the prefent *embargo act.* The reafon I felect *him* as the orator, is, that he is well verfed in Old Englifh Statutes, and will by that time have had a great deal of experience on the effects of this mild and humane act.

It would be entertaining to hear the learned judge contraft the liberality of *this act* with fome of the worft acts of the amiable Harry the VIIIth, or thofe fupporters of civil liberty, the Stuarts.

There was one advantage the Stuarts left, *open* to our anceftors, which is fhut up from us their defcendants.

When *they* were oppreffed they could migrate—they could quit the country.—The King never iffued a GENERAL "ne exeat regno." But our disfranchifing act prohibits the migration or departure of any man, woman or child even in neutral bottoms, without the *exprefs permiffion* of the Prefident.

Having made thefe few remarks not with the hope of drawing the attention of this *imprifoned nation* to the features of this act, much lefs with an expectation of kindling their refentment (for what can men do who have fubmitted willingly to have their hands and feet chained:)

Conftitution. But ftill *in theory* he is bound by his *own laws.* Now let us fee what *he* cannot *even permit* by this horrible fection.

The Prefident himfelf *cannot permit* any veffel to fail from Bofton to Newburyport, Portland, or round Cape Cod.

The *only* veffels which *can have* licenfes, or the enviable privilege of giving 9000 dollar bonds for a boat of 30 tons, are thofe which have *uniformly been* confined to bays, founds or rivers. Maffachufetts Bay is bounded at its two extremes by Race Point and Cape Ann.

Veffels that at any time, *even once* fince they were built, went to Newburyport, Portfmouth, Portland, or round the cape to Nantucket or Chatham, *cannot be licenfed* to go any where. Even thofe that never went out of the bay muft always remain there—they cannot therefore fupply the place of the Eaftern coafters which are *disfranchifed.*

A veffel which has been confined to Cafco bay, or Penobfcot bay may ply *freely there* on giving bond &c. but they cannot go over to any Ifland or bank to catch fifh out of the bay.

It may be faid this is too ludicrous. I can affure the public it is true. I know not how it will be conftrued by the Collector, but fuch is the *law.*

All our oyfters muft be brought by land becaufe no veffel can go

ters "the foldier;"—and to Lewis, friendfhip; tell him not to be difcouraged, he can never be fo fortunate in the profeffion as I have been.

" If the queftion of retaliation be decided without further acts of violence, I hope to fee you and your family, in the courfe of the winter; but it is carried to the extreme of ferocity, I have no hopes ever to fee my country, or friends again—Remember fweet little Marcia.

"Farewell—"Your faithful friend, —————."

Extract of a letter, dated Quebec Gaol, 17th November 1813.

"I am now in clofe confinement —my wandering limited by bolts, bars, and locks. So much for the inhuman operation of the unchriftian principle of RETALIATION. My unfortunate condition forbids to indulge in comment on the odious and ruinous features of retaliation; but to you, my friend, I cannot refrain for the expreffion of my regret for the eagernefs and avidity with which foreigners have been welcomed by the impolitic lenity of our laws. The beginning of the approaching cataftrophe, by which the proud American will be difgraced by the moft ignominious of deaths, is the adoption of foreigners as American citizens. The American, who, from affection and duty to his country, willingly yields his life to its fervice, muft feel the deepeft mor-

Another editorial in the *Salem Gazette* deploring the Embargo Act of 1813 and the closing of New England ports to enemy shipping. At the outbreak of the War of 1812, New England Federalist merchants were in a state of near-rebellion. They virtually boycotted the war effort, subscribed only reluctantly to national loans, moved their currency out of the country to Canada, and often provided supplies for the British fleet lying offshore.

imported in vessels not owned by citizens of the United States. The proceeds were specifically earmarked for a "Mediterranean war fund." The surtax was to continue until three months after a treaty of peace was signed. In 1815 Commodore Decatur and his tiny fleet defeated the Barbary powers. The Act of 1804 was extended until 1816 when peace was declared and the Barbary powers had made suitable restitution.

Early Smuggling

In the early days of the republic, just as now, smugglers, employing ingenious methods, were the bane of Customs. The detection and prevention of smuggling along the seaboard and the frontiers was a continuing challenge. Contemporary smugglers had accomplices among the citizenry, especially those who opposed the Tariff Act. By aiding and abetting smuggling, they felt they were being compensated for their objections by deliberately permitting the government to be defrauded out of its lawful revenues. This did not make the job of the Customs officers any simpler.

When Thomas Jefferson had succeeded in persuading the nation's lawmakers to pass the Embargo Act in 1807, his intention was to cut into Great Britain's valuable trade with the United States. But the legislation boomeranged, creating near-complete paralysis for industrialized New England and hostility in the states from Maine to Rhode Island. As if this were not enough, the "Land Embargo," enacted the following year, suspended Canadian border relations and caused great distress to New Englanders accustomed to marketing timber, potash, and other goods in Canada.

Smuggling by sea and land was inevitable and it was not long in coming. The Vermont border, close to the larger Canadian towns, was a natural base of operations for illegal traffic. U.S. Customs officers, sympathizing with their fellow citizens, were not overzealous in their enforcement of the law. Lawbreaking had been regarded as an act of patriotism only a generation earlier, and juries were reluctant to convict violators of the embargo.

The situation was so bad that the Vermont Customs Collector Jabez Penniman, in April 1808, notified Secretary of the Treasury Albert Gallatin that it was impossible to enforce the statutes without military aid. President Jefferson directed Gallatin to instruct the collector to engage and equip crews and arm as many vessels as necessary to enforce the law.

Alburg, located on a peninsula extending into Lake Champlain, was a perfect site for smuggling between the United States and Canada. Messengers, hired by Troy and Albany merchants to deliver foreign goods, would trudge through the thick woodlands with contraband strapped to their backs for deposit in an established hideaway near the border, to be carried by team or vessel to their destination. On one occasion, a Customs officer, intent on stopping the illegal imports, leaped aboard a Troy-bound smuggling craft, only to be tossed overboard and left standing chin-deep in the water. The staid New Englanders were aroused to such a state of anger that when the Vermont governor stationed troops at Alburg in May 1808, the lumber and potash merchants defiantly proclaimed they would carry on trade by armed force and would kill any Customs collector or other officer who attempted to enforce the laws.

It was not unusual for Canadians to devise a few schemes of their own, such as crossing the border and stowing away sums of money near the homesteads of American friends, with which they paid the "smugglers." Soon American farmers were missing horses, cattle, and swine, but their disappearance created neither excitement nor surprise. An even more ingenious plot was devised for loading wagons or sleds with New England produce and driving them along the border to the top of a nearby hill which sloped abruptly northward. There a crude hut was built and stocked with pork, barrels of flour, and other commodities. These shelters were so carefully designed that when a stone was removed from the foundation, the sides of the hut would collapse, the floor would give way, and the provisions would roll gently downhill into Canada. Senator Hillhouse of Connecticut asserted in a debate during November 1808 that "patriotism, cannon, militia, and all" had not stopped smuggling. A certain amount of it might have been curtailed along the lakes, but the inhabitants along the border, he said, were "cutting new roads to carry it on by land."

The smugglers were resourceful and daring in their exploits, resorting to force when necessary. One craft, The Black Snake, became notorious on Lake Champlain. Built originally as a ferry, forty feet long and seventeen feet wide, it was equipped with seven oars on each side and a sail. The vessel was smeared with black tar. A hundred barrels of potash, carried at the current high freight rate of $5 or $6 a barrel, made its operations extremely profitable. The boat was manned by a crew of powerful, well-armed men widely known as desperadoes. For months they scorned Customs officers and carried load after load across the border.

Government officials were determined to put an end to this traffic. On August 1, 1808, Lieutenant Farrington, Sergeant Johnson, and twelve infantry privates were detailed to the twelve-oared cutter, The Fly, with orders to pursue The Black Snake.

The smugglers remained in seclusion near shore during the day, but at night The Black Snake began to ply its way to the mouth of the Onion (now the Winooski) River. The men on board were armed with spike poles, large clubs, a basket of stones, and an eight-foot gun carrying fifteen bullets—all to fight off revenue boats. Rumors of the pursuit must have reached the armed crew members; they smuggled supplies of bullets all night to replenish their low supply of ammunition.

It was morning before the revenue officers sighted their quarry, about three miles up the river, made fast to the shore. Although the captain, Truman Mudgett, warned the federal officers not to touch The Black Snake, Lieutenant Farrington and several of his men climbed aboard to take possession of the vessel. During the struggle, three government men were killed and the lieutenant was wounded severely. At this point Sergeant Johnson and a detachment of troops made a determined last effort and captured all but two of the smugglers. Those two were arrested later and all were taken into custody.

State elections were imminent, and the members of the Federalist party, who were against the embargo, were charged with attempting to shield the murderers. Inflammatory handbills, printed with pictures of three coffins, were circulated.

Less than three weeks after *The Black Snake* episode, the Vermont Supreme Court convened in special session at Burlington and indicted eight men for the killing of the three government officials. Three of the eight were found guilty. Two weeks later Cyrus B. Dean, the one man sentenced to be hanged, was hauled to the courthouse to listen to a sermon before he was executed before a crowd of 10,000.

Two other men, convicted of manslaughter, were sentenced to stand one hour in the pillory, receive fifty lashes each on the bare back, and serve ten years in the state prison.

These trials, held during a time of bitter political strife, were among the most famous in the history of Vermont jurisprudence—when the hardships of the embargo bore heavily upon all classes of people, and smuggling was still considered respectable by many.

The War of 1812, with its embargoes and stringent regulation of shipping, thrust additional burdens on Customs officers. In spite of the efforts of some courageous Customs officers, smuggling during the War of 1812 was extensive. The British Army, in desperate need of provisions, often stole across the Vermont border and paid high prices for American cattle.

Revenue officers and militiamen were usually successful in their pursuit of

The passenger manifest of the vessel *Cadmus*, arriving at New York on August 17, 1824. The names of General LaFayette and that of his son appear on the list.

A passport of 1838, intended to ensure the safe passage of a ship and its entire crew.

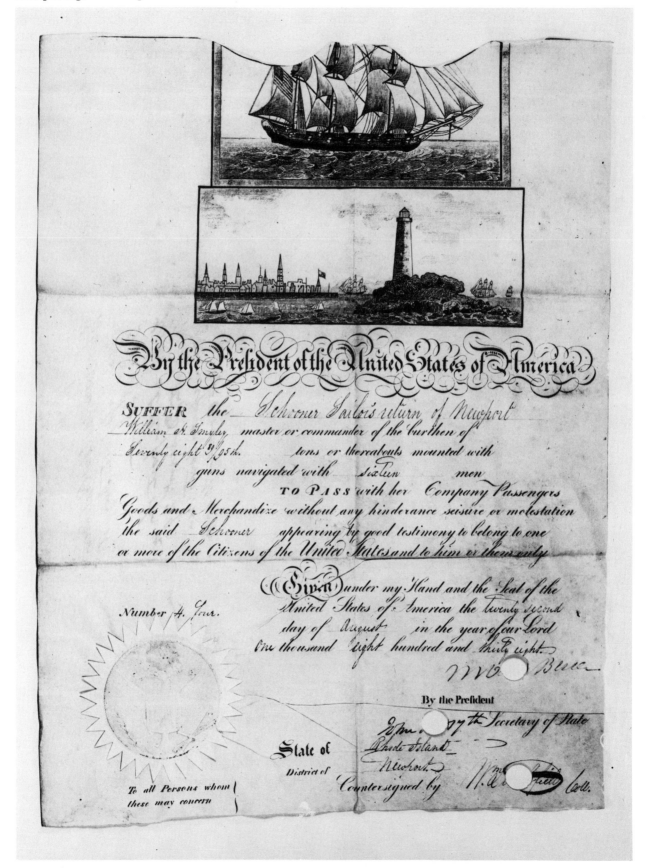

Canadian-bound drivers, turning team after team of horses hauling merchandise en route to Montreal back to Boston.

The Governor General of Canada wrote to the British Foreign Office in August 1814 that "Two-thirds of the Army in Canada are at this moment eating beef provided by American contractors, principally from the States of Vermont and New York." An American general wrote: "Like herds of buffalos, they [cattle] pass through the forests, making paths for themselves. Were it not for these supplies, the British forces in Canada would soon be suffering from famine."

The early 1800s were bitter years, especially in the history of New England and the U.S. Customs Service. Woodrow Wilson's comment on the Embargo Act, almost a century later, echoed the pessimism of the period:

> The States themselves suffered from the act more than the nations. . . . America's own trade was ruined. Ships rotted at the Wharves—the ships which had but yesterday carried the commerce of the world. The quays were deserted. Nothing would sell any more at its old price. . . . No vigilance or compulsion could really enforce the act. . . . Smuggling took the place of legitimate trade where it could.

With the passage of the first Tariff Act, it was hoped that collections would yield $3,000,000 of the $8,000,000 immediately needed for the operation of the new government. During the first year of the act, only about $2,240,000 was realized, plus an additional $157,000 in duties on tonnage. From year to year, Customs receipts steadily increased with the growth of the nation, until in 1929, they amounted to over $600,000,000. Today, they are nearing $4.5 billion.

At one time the entire peacetime expenditures of the government amounted to much less than a billion dollars a year and, up to 1910, Customs duties constituted the principal single source of the government's income. However, with the advent of a billion-dollar budget, it became apparent that new sources of revenue would have to be found. The income tax of 1913 was the result, and today that source of revenue, combined with other federal income, pays for the lion's share of the national budget.

By 1852 the Customs Service had reached a high state of development as that branch of the government dealing with all matters relating to imports, exports, and shipping. For nearly half a century there had been no legislation affecting the organization of the agency, except for a few minor laws that added to its responsibilities or slightly modified the activities of its officers.

The Civil War apparently had little direct effect upon the operations of the service. Special controls were issued governing exports, but industrial development and the government's war needs did not necessitate the same degree of controls on imports and exports that were to be put into effect during the war with Germany half a century later.

The Spoils System

While our earliest presidents made some appointments to public office on the basis of qualifications or previous service, it soon became accepted practice in

SEARCHING A SUSPECTED SMUGGLER.

An old newspaper print purporting to show
the apprehension of a smuggler, perhaps a
hundred years ago.

Matthew A. Henson, as the Arctic explorer
who accompanied Admiral Peary to the
North Pole, and later as a Customs employee
in New York.

political appointments that "to the victor belong the spoils." By 1841 the spoils system had reached such proportions that when William Henry Harrison became President, from 30,000 to 40,000 office seekers swarmed into the capital to claim the 23,700 jobs in the federal executive service.

There were four categories of political appointees in the Customs Service: collectors, comptrollers, appraisers, and surveyors, all of whom served at the pleasure of the administration in office. Ironically, a century later, in 1927, the Commissioner of Customs, their chief, was technically outranked by the appointees under his supervision. Some of them never let it be forgotten that they were protégés of powerful congressmen or senators and were not averse to ignoring or openly defying instructions from bureau headquarters in Washington. Others did their homework, worked hard for Customs, and eventually became career supervisors.

Defiance and inertia were the least of the problems spawned by the political appointees. Many simply were incapable of performing their duties. Charged with responsibility for "dealing with the public and taking the complaints in handling of entries and liquidations," their hands were tied by a lack of knowledge and lack of authority. Responsible for "encouraging overall commerce," they were incapable of explaining and interpreting Customs regulations. In "providing overall management," they had no yardstick for evaluating their efforts or making proper use of existing resources.

The collectors' presence meant that two persons had to be hired to perform the

This Prohibition era photograph shows one of the more impractical methods used to smuggle whiskey.

same job. The assistant collectors became the technicians, the career civil servants who performed the actual routine daily work of Customs.

By 1853 it had become the custom to stop all regular work for a month after the inauguration so that the President and the heads of the departments could settle the many and conflicting claims of the spoilsmen.

The spoils system was still an entrenched feature of government when President Lincoln took office. With the country in one of its gravest crises, Lincoln refused, after his second election, to abide by the "rotation theory," the main strength of the spoils system, and he appointed officials from the opposition party.

President Ulysses S. Grant, elected on a platform that included a promise of Civil Service reform, took office in 1869 and was able to appoint a Civil Service Commission by attaching a last-minute rider to an appropriation bill.

By the end of the Civil War, the spoils system was firmly controlled and organized by the major political parties and was to remain so for a century. Every time the opposition party came into power, employees' heads would roll and their replacements were appointed on the basis of how much they had done for the party in power. Experience, expertise, diligence, and loyalty counted for little. The dishing out of patronage persisted to some degree even at mid-management levels in the federal bureaucracy for many years.

In the administration of Andrew Johnson, the entire executive branch of gov-

An early Customs office in Montana. In the territories and the western states, the collector of Customs was often the first federal officer on the scene.

Four of the many buildings that, over the
years, served as customhouses in San
Francisco.

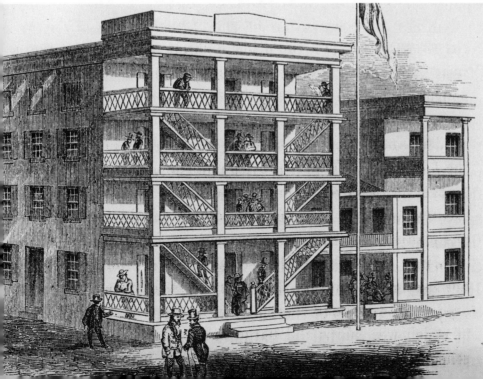

ernment, consisting of 53,000 employees (compared with 2.5 million in 1975) with a payroll of $30 million annually (compared with $2.5 billion today), dispensed patronage through the Post Office Department, the Treasury Department, the Interior Department, the Patent Office, the Bureau of Indian Affairs, the Pension Bureau, the War, Navy, State, and Justice departments. During the Lincoln administration, out of a total of 1,639 presidential positions, 1,457 individuals were removed and replaced.

The country's largest single office in the Executive Branch of the federal government was the customhouse in New York City which, in 1877, collected $108,000,000 or three-quarters of the nation's total customs revenue. It was the country's greatest source of patronage, and both parties, Republican and Democratic, scrambled for jobs in the customhouse.

This old streetcar was converted to a
Customs office in Texas.

Looming over the nation's greatest customhouse like a colossus was the collector, described by Hartman in *Politics and Patronage* as the "symbol of the Spoilsman, running a political machine, sacrificing the needs of the community as a whole to the selfish ends of factional politics." The collector would make appointments and dismissals virtually without controls or supervision, deftly levying the traditional 2 percent annual assessment on his employees for the political party's coffers.

By mid-century, tributes, assessments, and other fees netted the average Customs collector an annual income of $30,000. When Chester A. Arthur, the most famous collector in American history, was appointed to that office by President Ulysses Grant, his salary of $50,000 equaled that of the Chief Executive himself.

That the control of Civil Service employees by professional politicians was a threat to democratic government, while it debased and degraded the American political system, was increasingly recognized. A wide spectrum of publications, from *The Nation* to *The New York Times* and *Harper's Weekly,* demanded Civil Service reform, permitting qualified and trained persons to remain in their positions. On May 11, 1876, *The Nation* in an editorial by E. L. Godkin, bellowed that the Civil Service "includes almost every evil of which the American people have at this moment to complain. The seat of all fraud and corruption and infidelity and inefficiency and negligence is to be found in it."

The Customs House in Buffalo, New York, built in 1858, here photographed just before its demolition in 1965.
Courtesy the *Buffalo Evening News.*

A special Revenue Investigative Commission, which had been appointed by President Andrew Johnson, reported earlier in 1866 that the government was being cheated out of up to $25 million annually through corruption at the New York Customhouse. Pressure for reform mounted, with support from the press and the public.

The beginning of the end of the spoils system came in 1881 when Charles Guiteau, agitated by a patronage dispute, slipped up behind President Garfield in a Washington railroad station and shot the President in the back. This tragedy aroused public opinion to such an extent that Congress passed the Civil Service Act, establishing the principle that persons privileged to serve the American people in government career posts should be selected on the basis of merit.

In the eleven attempts that had been made from 1912 to 1965 to abolish political appointees in Customs, 137 positions were either eliminated or brought under the competitive Civil Service umbrella. President William Howard Taft made a serious attempt to rid Customs of patronage, but his party's leadership needed the jobs and they weren't inclined to give up this leverage. Under one of the Reorganization Acts of 1912, Taft succeeded in eliminating a number of patronage positions in Customs. Six years later, the Tariff Commission recommended further reform, but no action was taken. In 1932 the Treasury eliminated the obsolete posts of surveyors and appraisers of merchandise, except in New York, thus further reducing the number of presidential appointees.

In 1937, a report of the President's Committee on Administrative Management stated: "The continued appointment by the President of field officials, such as . . . Collectors of Customs, is not only antiquated, but prejudicial to good administration." No action was taken. Patronage was seemingly there to stay.

In 1939 and 1943 renewed efforts were made to cleanse the Customs Service of patronage jobs, but only the unfilled post of comptroller at San Francisco was abolished. In 1947 a detailed management survey urged that all supervisory positions in Customs be filled with career employees. The survey argued that top positions required technical knowledge, that the presidentially appointed commissioner was hampered when subordinates were appointed and dismissed by another arm of government, that the division of responsibility between the presidential appointee and the assistant collector, the latter a technician, drastically reduced effectiveness; and that two men were doing a one-man job, at considerable cost to the taxpayer.

Another blow to the patronage system, which also struck at the Internal Revenue Service, was made in 1949 by the Hoover Commission, which observed dryly: "These appointments are regarded by some as sinecures. In any event, they form a bar to orderly development of an experienced staff." But in 1952, 1957, and 1959 fresh purge attempts were turned down by Congress.

It was not until 1965—fifty-three years after William Howard Taft's opening sally—that the ax dropped and the Customs Service was at long last converted into an all-career service, thanks to the steady, relentless pressure and insistence of Commissioner Nichols. Out of consideration for the feelings of the incumbent appointees, they were given the opportunity to remain on the federal payroll for

Two 1880 newspaper woodcuts showing the
Customs inspection of arriving passengers
and commenting on the public's general
attitude toward the inspectors.

FRANK LESLIE'S ILLUSTRATED NEWSPAPER.   [November 27, 1880.]

MAKING DECLARATIONS

RETURNING CHECKS.

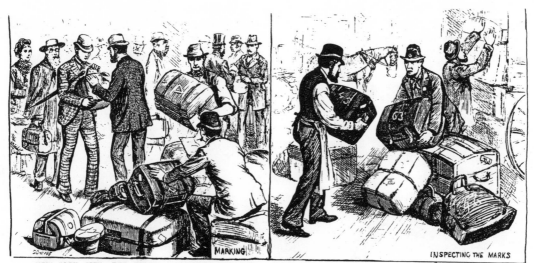

MARKING

INSPECTING THE MARKS

NEW YORK CITY.—THE TERROR OF OCEAN TRAVELERS—A DAY WITH A CUSTOM HOUSE INSPECTOR.

three years, with new titles: "program advisors." Several of the collectors who
had performed their work satisfactorily applied for career positions as district
directors in Customs. Others just faded into oblivion. The combined salaries for

Customhouse employees and the offices they worked in around the turn of the century in San Francisco.

Merchandise from the appraisers' stores,
San Francisco, circa 1930.

the fifty-three presidential appointees for a single year had been $1 million. The Collectors of Customs have passed into oblivion.

World War I drastically broadened the activities of the Customs Service. Prior to United States entry into the war, Customs officers, in addition to their regular duties, were charged with enforcement of the neutrality laws at the country's ports and harbors. This demanded the exercise of extreme vigilance to prevent the equipping of hostile expeditions in American waters, or the use of American ports as bases for supplying belligerent warships. Customs officers had to learn to perform hazardous and exhausting jobs. They were busy sealing the wireless apparatus of vessels while in U.S. ports; inspecting suspicious cargoes; and investigating attempts to damage and destroy vessels and their cargoes.

Hidalgo, Texas, a ramshackle border town, photographed in 1916. The customhouse can be seen in the background.

When the United States entered World War I on April 6, 1917, Customs officers, on instructions from President Wilson, took into custody sixty-five German warships anchored at seventeen different ports, and posted twenty-four-hour guards to protect them from destruction and deterioration. On April 9, fourteen Austrian ships at eight U.S. ports were placed under Customs custody. War Trade Board regulations called for Customs officers to enforce the policy requiring the licensing of wartime imports and exports and the checking of all shipments entering and leaving the country. Customs officers made detailed examinations of passengers and baggage leaving the country and exercised a stringent censorship on motion picture films, photographic negatives, letters, and other communications.

Because of its organization and experience, the Customs Service was designated the agency best adapted to enforce the Espionage Act of June 15, 1917, and the Trading with the Enemy Act of October 6, 1917, both of which required intensive examination of outgoing and incoming passengers and ships. Thus, the Customs Intelligence Bureau (CIB) was created—a band of 260 hand-picked men from the staff at the New York Customhouse.

The Port of New York became the key staging area for the country's war effort. The office of the Customs collector at New York became so important that Byron R. Newton, who had been serving as assistant secretary of the treasury, was relieved of his job and reassigned as collector in New York.

By 1918 the volume of work had become so great that a much larger force was needed. In April, the Treasury Department authorized the hiring of 300 temporary workers at $4 a day. Newspaper advertisements urged those men who were exempt from the draft or in deferred categories to "do their patriotic duty" and serve with Customs in protecting the Port of New York. Thousands responded, but only 300 could be hired. Each man was called before a committee and subjected to intensive questioning, followed by a thorough physical examination. Men who were fluent in more than one foreign language were especially in demand.

The hired force cut across a broad spectrum of society. They had a varied educational background, from elementary school to university training. There was even a former boxer, whose huge bulk and unfailing courtesy made him invaluable in maintaining order.

Morale must have been high; a report states that most of the group showed "a most commendable spirit of the highest degree of loyalty. They cheerfully accepted assignment to the most arduous tasks, giving the best that was in them as their contribution to the Nation in the hour of its need."

The CIB was organized into sections, headed by a first lieutenant and a second lieutenant, and into squads or platoons, consisting of a sergeant and seven corporals or searchers. The men of the CIB had many duties. They issued certificates of citizenship to American seamen; they mustered the crews of all incoming vessels to establish their identity, issued identification cards, and authorized shore leave. They guarded vessels to prevent persons from landing or boarding without permits. When ships were ready to depart, the men of the CIB again mustered the crews to insure that no unauthorized persons went aboard.

This ramshackle building served as a customhouse in the state of Washington from 1917 to 1936.
Courtesy of Werner Lenggenhager.

The magnificent Customs House at Bowling Green in lower Manhattan, put into service in 1907 and now designated an historic landmark.

Each day the cutter section of the CIB checked in at the information unit before going down the bay, and received a set of suspect books to be used in checking crews. They inspected and stamped the passports of all persons departing from the United States, and they maintained surveillance of tugs, motorboats, and other small craft to prevent acts of sabotage.

The CIB members were outfitted in olive drab coats, trousers, overcoats, caps, and overalls, with a yearly clothing allowance of $120 that also had to cover equipment and "to compensate for additional expense incurred in performance of special duties."

The Customs Intelligence Bureau was not without casualties. At least one searcher died from injuries received by falling down the hatchway of a ship. Several succumbed to disease caused by exposure. During the influenza epidemic of October 1918, a group of searchers had to board a disease-ridden ship and inspect the crew and their germ-laden effects over a period of fourteen hours. During the operation, a noisy procession of ambulances was carrying the sick and dying to nearby hospitals. One report pays glowing tribute to the men of the CIB. "Though the large number of officers engaged in this operation were warned of the facts and attendant dangers, not a man flinched," it said.

The Customs Intelligence Bureau was disbanded when the war ended. It received a group citation from the secretary of war and the secretary of the treasury. In July 1919 the temporary officers were mustered out and awarded certificates similar to the discharges granted members of the Armed Forces.

In the old customhouse at Bowling Green, New York City, which was abandoned in 1973, there hung an oversize photograph of the 286 men of the CIB taken in Battery Park near what is now known as Castle Clinton National Monument. Edward R. Norwood, former Supervising Customs Agent at Tampa, was Chief of the CIB.

The Customs Border Patrol

The original Customs Border Patrol was organized in 1853, when Secretary of the Treasury Samuel Casey authorized Customs collectors to hire inspectors for horseback patrol duty along the borders. As late as 1916 the patrolmen were paid only a few dollars a day. They were required to supply, at their own expense, two pistols, a rifle, a pony, and a pack mule.

The first collector to hire inspectors for mounted duty was Caleb Sherman in El Paso. In the early years of the Civil War the activities of Customs' new mounted force were curtailed along the southwestern border because the Confederates held much of the territory. From 1853 to 1933, Border Patrol officers reported to local Customs collectors and were called, simply, "mounted inspectors." In 1933 they were given the title of "Customs Port Inspector (CPI)," and in 1936 they came under the jurisdiction of the Customs investigative division.

After the Civil War it wasn't long before the mounted inspectors were back on the job. Their work was seldom dull. One wrote, "In recent months the mail has been captured by bad Indians between Tucson and El Paso. New men on the force are warned that any duty money they send to headquarters is sent at the carrier's own risk."

During the life-span of the Patrol, authority for hiring members seesawed between collectors and Civil Service officials in Washington. Until 1894, collectors were permitted to hire without regard for Washington's regulations. Between 1894 and 1906, however, applicants had to meet Civil Service requirements, but after 1906 collectors were again permitted to hire men of their choice. The eased requirements for membership in the patrol force ultimately proved beneficial to Customs. They encouraged men with little formal education but much law enforcement experience to sign on as mounted inspectors. Some of these men were veteran lawmen, former Texas Rangers and ex-sheriffs, who had been in the famed First U.S. Volunteer Cavalry, better known today as Teddy Roosevelt's Rough Riders.

A scant thirteen years after the former Rough Riders augmented the Customs mounted patrol force, Representative A. J. Volstead persuaded Congress to outlaw the manufacture and sale of alcoholic beverages. The Prohibition era began, and it didn't take shrewd criminals long to see that a lot of money could be made by supplying thirsty Americans with illegal liquor, both homemade and smuggled.

In the years when the law was in effect, from 1919 to 1933, Customs' mounted inspectors and many other federal and local lawmen battled bootleggers on both borders in a futile effort to enforce the Volstead Act.

Then as today, the smugglers' ingenuity knew few limits. "They used to use every trick in the book to slip liquor into the country," says Fred W. Maguire, who served in the mounted force on both borders during his Customs career. "They used boats with false decks that concealed countless gallons of liquor lashed down in the concealed areas.

"One bunch in Michigan had a real clever scheme going," Maguire recalled. "They made a long, torpedolike metal cylinder, waterproofed it, filled it with liquor, and pulled it across a lake on the border by using a long steel cable. They submerged the cylinder five feet below the surface, and only used it at night. One of our men spotted the rig glistening on a clear moonlit night.

"Every trip brought fifteen more gallons into the country. By the time we arrested the men, they had thousands of gallons of bootleg liquor stored and awaiting sale."

Another Prohibition veteran is J. F. Weadock, who wrote in 1966 about the honesty of Customs personnel during that era of violence and bribery. He also wrote of the men on the mounted force and the job they were hired to do. "It is to the everlasting credit of the service that few men who wore the Customs badge succumbed to the lure of easy money which was offered them," he wrote. "In fact, when one man did succumb, he was soon detected by the men he worked with. His chief showed personal hurt when he had to turn the man over to the Justice Department."

Writing about his co-workers and the near-impossible job they were hired to do, Weadock said, "These were men who were called on to enforce Prohibition along a border so rough and isolated it would have taken a small army to do the job. Later, as other men joined forces with Customs, the mileage to be covered still made full enforcement a joke to the men on the line. The law, written and conceived by men in easy chairs in well-appointed offices far from the border, had little in common with the conditions under which it had to be enforced."

Mounted Customs inspector Robert Stuart Rumsey was only one of many early border patrol officers to lose their lives in the performance of their duties. Rumsey was shot and killed while attempting to apprehend whiskey smugglers along the Mexican border.

The Prohibition era was a violent one. Records indicate that some forty Customs officers were killed by criminals, mostly along the Mexican border. Yet, the Patrol officers apparently kept their balance. One even cared for the dog of a smuggler he had arrested, while the culprit was in jail.

Some members of the force spent their days (and nights) in boats keeping surveillance on the Great Lakes or along the Gulf Coast. Claude Blancq, Jr., who retired in 1962 as Assistant Regional Commissioner in New Orleans, tells a story about liquor smuggling by boat. It involves his father, who had been chief of the New Orleans District vessel documentation section.

"On one occasion Prohibition agents captured a boat deep in the bayou. They posted a guard overnight and the next morning my father was sent with a crew to bring it back. The boat was so heavily loaded it could not get past some shallow waters. Something had to go. My father ordered part of the cargo jettisoned. Somewhere in the marshes of Louisiana, unless a lucky fisherman has found them, are 500 fifths of good old Prohibition rotgut."

After 1932 the hiring of mounted patrol inspectors again had to conform to Civil Service requirements. In 1936, after the force was absorbed by the Customs investigative division, patrol inspector districts were created in four locations: Buffalo, N.Y.; Jacksonville, Fla.; El Paso, Texas; and Havre, Mont.

After Congressman Volstead's unpopular act was repealed in 1933, federal lawmen found out that liquor smuggling was continuing at nearly the same level as before. Many Americans continued to buy smuggled liquor because it was lower priced and often of better quality than the beverages available legally after 1933. The enthusiastic consumption of contraband "spirits" kept Customs busy. During a 1934 meeting of Customs collectors, Saul Haas from Seattle and John Tulloch from Ogdensburg told Commissioner J. H. Moyle in very definite language that their men were still chasing liquor smugglers. Summing up, Tulloch said: "Just as long as the bootlegger is able to furnish better and cheaper liquor than legal dealers, we are going to have to cope with him."

During World War II, Customs port inspectors investigated other types of smuggling, as well as the usual narcotics, gold, and jewelry. Such normally easy-

Patrolling along the country's northern border presents some special problems in the winter, and Customs officers have had to use snowshoes, modified motorcycles, and bizarre-looking, propeller-driven snowmobiles to perform their duty.

to-get items as tires, silk, stockings, steaks, and sugar became scarce and were smuggled on both borders.

Two factors led to the end of the mounted inspector force. One was the postwar trade boom that placed new strains on Customs' manpower and budget resources. The other was the development of modern transportation, which reduced the strategic value of a horseback force, although a few mounted officers remained for specialized investigative work.

As early as 1917, smugglers had begun to see the possibilities of using automobiles. While mounted inspectors had to follow routes with watering holes for their horses, motorized smugglers could go by many different routes, farther and faster.

Between the first and second world wars, Customs transported men and horses by car and trailer as far as the roads went. There the inspectors mounted up and rode out to even more remote areas.

By 1947, however, the handwriting was on the wall. The increasing use of fast cars, sprawling new highways, and the growing popularity of private planes had made the mounted inspector force little more than a relic of an unmechanized age. The Patrol was disbanded in 1948.

For a brief time in the 1970s Customs border patrol officers still worked on horseback, keeping alive a tradition that predates the Civil War. Here an officer keeps watch for smugglers along the Rio Grande near Brownsville, Texas.

In 1972 action was taken by Commissioner Vernon D. Acree to restore the highly mobile patrol force. In order to avoid confusion with Immigration border patrols, he named these groups "Tactical Interdiction Units." The border patrol of the Immigration and Naturalization Service was created by the Justice Department, and its primary responsibility was the interception of illegal aliens trying to get into the U.S.A.

Customs began using horses again in very limited numbers only because they enabled patrol officers to range farther and longer, and in areas where vehicles could not penetrate. When horses became obsolete, Customs changed with the times and today is equipped with the most sophisticated technology in the world. A few patrolmen use horses on rare occasions, when vehicles or helicopters are impractical.

chapter five

Modernization of the Customs Service

The organizational entity known as Customs was only a division within the Treasury Department until 1927, when Congress elevated it to the level of a bureau, with a commissioner theoretically in charge of operations. In actual fact, the collectors and appraisers under the commissioner were virtually independent, ruling over their districts without instructions, policy guidance, or help from Washington for several decades. By 1947 things began to change slowly and the commissioners soon were assuming authority over the field staff little by little. Unlike several other Treasury Department bureau chiefs, the commissioner was not a presidential appointee, although he seldom was designated without White House approval. This reflected the feeling in Congress that the job of Commissioner of Customs was simply not intended to be a position of great influence or importance in the governmental superstructure. The commissioner of Customs was not even invited to attend the weekly staff meetings held by the secretary of the treasury. An assistant secretary represented the interests of the Customs Service. Vernon D. Acree, after a year in office, was finally permitted in 1973 to attend Secretary George Shultz's Friday morning staff meetings, a breakthrough of sorts in the snaillike progress of Customs in receiving the recognition it had certainly earned in its 185 years of service to the United States. One astute observer stated:

That the incumbent [Commissioner of Customs] was not intended to be a power of the first magnitude may be deduced from the fact that no provision was made for his appointment by the President, or confirmation by the Senate. This is the rule of thumb line dividing the potentates from the peons.

The first four commissioners of Customs were Ernest W. Camp, appointed by Treasury Secretary Andrew W. Mellon, who served from 1927 to 1929; Francis X. A. Eble, also a Mellon appointee, who served from 1929 to 1933; James H. Moyle,

Ernest W. Camp, Commissioner of Customs
from 1927 to 1929.

Francis X. A. Eble, Commissioner of
Customs from 1929 to 1933.

James H. Moyle, Commissioner of Customs
from 1933 to 1939.

named by Secretary William H. Woodin, in office from 1933 to 1939, and Basil Harris, a Morgenthau appointee, commissioner from 1939 to 1940.

Although these four were doubtless men of integrity, their contribution to the advancement and development of Customs could hardly be described as momentous or even memorable. It was the fifth in the line of succession, W. R. Johnson, who can be said to have launched the Customs Service on its long, tortuous road toward "modernization." If any position in the executive branch of government warranted a presidential appointee at its head, it was the Bureau of Customs. But by a strange historical irony, this appointee of Henry Morgenthau, Jr., on July 19, 1940, instead of winning the accolades that were undeniably due him, enjoyed the dubious distinction of being the one and only commissioner in Customs history to be removed involuntarily from his position, after a hearing which amounted to an impeachment trial. He was reduced to a lesser job in the bureau hierarchy. Yet he was an outstanding administrator and made an outstanding contribution.

As a youth, Johnson left his native Colorado for New York City, where he landed a job first as a clerk, then as a "liquidator" in the old customhouse on Bowling Green. His work was to collate the reports of Customs inspectors, examiners, gaugers, chemists, and so forth and to assess the duties owing for each entry of imported merchandise. Liquidators, working at enormous tables piled high with documents totally incomprehensible to anyone not involved, had to possess a clear and detailed understanding of everything that had been done by all the other employees. The liquidators dug into their mountains of paper with their coats off, green eyeshades in place, and pencils poised over myriads of complex figures, doing at a snail's pace work that today is performed by computers and automatic data processing equipment in a fraction of the time, and with fewer people.

Realizing that he needed a law degree to climb the federal career ladder, Johnson attended night school and eventually became a member of the bar. His skill as a liquidator attracted the attention of the New York collector. This eventually led to his appointment at the age of thirty-five as chief counsel at bureau headquarters in Washington. Eventually he was named commissioner.

W. R. Johnson was considered by his peers as the finest legal draftsman ever to grace the Customs Service. One of his successors, Philip Nichols, Jr., who worked with him, recalls that:

> He could sit at a conference saying little until some proposal seemed to have acquiescence. Then he would grasp pen and paper, write a few words in his strong flowing script, and pass them around, saying, "Is this what you want?" It would go right to the working heart of a regulation or ruling,—succinct, clear, devoid of ambiguity. There would be none of the fumbling around, interlining, scratching out, and erasing, that most of us lawyers cannot avoid in course of the task, even when, eventually, the end product of our labor is acceptable. His proposed wording would make a good idea look better, and on the other hand, if the idea was bad, the draft would demolish it in a gale of laughter, beyond the possibility of repair.

In the second place, Johnson could explain at a moment's notice any part of the vast structure of statutes, regulations, and court decisions, old and new, that covered the operation of the U.S. Customs, clearly and accurately, without straining the listener's patience with irrelevant or boring detail, and without even a moment's hesitation or uncertainty. Johnson was incapable of appearing uncertain of anything.

Johnson did not merely build a paper structure of words and concepts. He literally launched the old line agency on its path toward modernization by setting forth how each provision of the Tariff Act *controlled* and *guided* the day-to-day work of the humblest Customs employee at the bottom of the career ladder—for the first time in history, establishing the basis for a job description and classification system that has prevailed in all federal Civil Service structures.

Johnson's great strength was his unique ability to manipulate the intractable mass of Customs regulations, squeezing from it answers to every problem. When Johnson indicated that the law required such and such a course of action, many

As these pictures illustrate, a recurring problem for Customs is the attempt to smuggle arms in and out of the country. This may involve the exporting of automatic and semiautomatic weapons and ammunition, or the importing of "Saturday night specials" and military "souvenirs" that still contain live explosives.

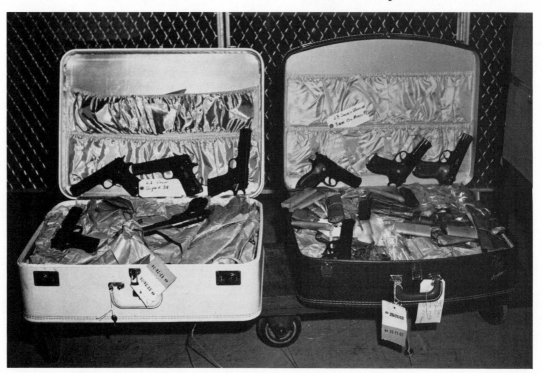

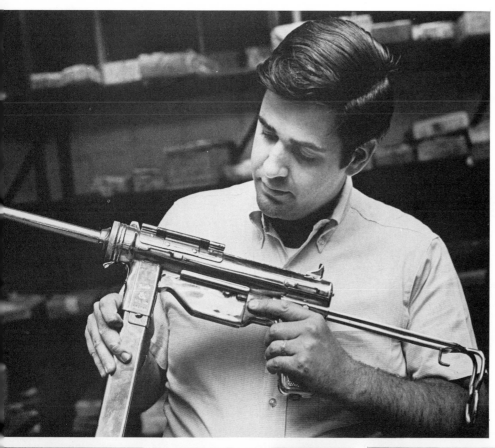

openly challenged him, doubting that the law was all that clear in its command. Some would refute Johnson with citations, but his stonewall logic eventually prevailed.

During his seven years as commissioner, Johnson was known for his rigid adherence to the letter of the law, as interpreted by himself. In actual fact he wore two hats, one as Customs commissioner and the other as chief of rule-making and interpretation, a function which really belonged to the chief counsel. One of the legends told about Johnson states that during World War II, when Canadian troops were sent to defend Alaska, Johnson insisted upon collecting customs duties on their arms and equipment. Johnson's own comment on this was that any fool should have known the story was false, because the arms and equipment of friendly foreign military contingents are not subject to customs duties by law. Out of curiosity, a Customs official, who shall remain unnamed, confirmed this fact but indicated that it was not spelled out anywhere in the Tariff Act until many years later. "It was then," he said, "one of the esoteric orchids of Customs law, that only the knowledgeable could find in the vast swamp of Customs jurisprudence."

Foreign lottery tickets are prohibited from entering the United States. This package of Irish Sweepstake tickets was seized by an alert Customs inspector in Jersey City.

The end of World War II resulted in a budget cut for the Customs Service. Although the cut was a relatively small one, ordered by the House Appropriations Committee and subject to Senate approval, W. R. Johnson, as always, responsive to the mood of Congress, failed to appeal. Instead, he welcomed the opportunity to cooperate in helping the new Republican majority to keep its preelection promises. He knew exactly how to absorb the cut. That very day, he sent out telegrams abolishing the Northern Customs Border Patrol.

This was an absurdly small handful of men, considering the magnitude of their mission, with little equipment and training, who guarded the long common border with Canada. An arm of the patrol was permitted to survive a little while longer, but it was common knowledge that the Customs patrolmen only duplicated the work of the larger and better equipped Immigration Service as border guards. Ports of entry were basically the responsibility of deputy collectors and their inspector staffs. But the capability of the investigative arm—known as the Customs Agency Service—with its own techniques for combating smuggling, was of a high order. The elimination of the Customs patrolmen along the Canadian-U.S. border was therefore thought to be of no real significance in the effort to interdict drugs.

W. R. Johnson, however, had no experience in coping with the federal employee whose job had been abolished. Although his intentions were honorable, and his integrity unassailable, he was simultaneously the target for angry letters and telegrams which flooded the halls of Congress protesting the reduction in jobs, and for congressional fury on the grounds that he had fomented the citizen "rebellion." Besides the barrage of mail and the tornado of speeches which swept Congress, mass meetings demanding that Congress "Stop That Axe," and mass marches down Pennsylvania Avenue in Washington, aroused legislators to a new pitch of anger against the "Bureaucracy."

To the House Appropriations Subcommittee, W. R. Johnson became the living symbol of rebellious federal employees. One up-and-coming Member of the House from Massachusetts, Christian A. Herter, made clear his feelings in a scalding article in the September 1947 edition of the Reader's Digest:

> Bureaucracy's tactics in this fight for continued expansion [of the federal payroll] probably reached a record low in the Customs Bureau. Here is an essential Bureau which, last year, spent 20% more than in the previous year. It came to us asking for a further increase of 22%.
>
> Extended House hearings and a subsequent Senate investigation revealed that the Bureau was badly in need of overhauling. Its spokesman presented to Congress at least three separate financial estimates of its operating deficit, each differing from the other by a sizable amount. Many of its top administrators—Collectors and Comptrollers of Customs—were found, according to a Senate report, to be *unqualified for the work, irregular in attendance at their office. Their claims to their position are purely political.* Four were at least 80 years of age and "physically incapable of carrying out their duties." One was a practicing physician "who visited the Customs office about once in two weeks—presumably on paydays."

Herter then charged W. R. Johnson with conduct which fell short of treason by a hair's breadth.

When that blow at bureaucratic expansion fell, the Commissioner of Customs, openly blaming Congress, dramatically laid off 85% of all officers charged with the essential job of guarding our ports and borders against smugglers and narcotics traffickers.
  Long stretches of our borders were left totally unpatrolled. Only skeleton staffs remained to protect many of our port cities. No one else was laid off—not one stenographer, office boy or clerk; only those whose layoff would quickly impair the most important work of the bureau and thus most readily serve to arouse the public.

At the Committee hearings, W. R. Johnson's version of his motives in dissolving the Border Patrol received little credence or support. Members of Congress felt that Johnson had acted precipitously; that he had overreacted to the call for budget cuts, that he had not consulted the secretary of the treasury, that he failed to await the result of a Senate appeal, and that he had acted without advice from his own budget officer, David Strubinger.
  Johnson was found "guilty" and Treasury Secretary John W. Snyder received orders to remove him from the post of Commissioner. Snyder was a decent and honorable man but he had been appointed to the Cabinet by President Truman, and he had no desire to protect Treasury Secretary Henry Morgenthau's appointees from their own folly. And so Johnson was fired. But instead of going off the payroll, he was reduced to a position one step below the commissioner, a job that had been created by Johnson himself with remarkable foresight. And inasmuch as he was a career civil servant, with permanent status and rights, Secretary Snyder, to his everlasting credit, permitted him to remain.
  The new commissioner, Frank Dow, another career man with even more years of service than Johnson, succeeded to the commissionership on June 29, 1949, just about two years after Johnson's dismissal. Dow hailed from the state of Maine, and was a man of hard common sense and salty speech who managed to serve with no problems on the Hill or with anyone in the trading community.

Frank Dow, Commissioner of Customs from 1949 to 1953.

As for Johnson, in his new position he still reserved unto himself the same privilege of interpreting regulations, a function in which he had no equal and one which he always loved. Commissioner Frank Dow was only too happy to have a man like Johnson on his staff. He happily deferred to him on whatever decisions were recommended by Johnson, for whose encyclopedic knowledge Customs men everywhere had the profoundest respect. And so Johnson remained an intellectual powerhouse in the bureau headquarters for years.

But Johnson's troubles were not over. Because of an honest difference of opinion on a legal matter, a fellow employee brought new charges against him. One of the charges was to the effect that Johnson was using secretarial help for "personal" purposes; i.e., compiling a monumental book of information entitled *Johnson on Tariff Classification.* But it was needed in the Customs Service badly, and the matter was dropped.

Ultimately, Johnson was retained by an important New York law firm specializing in Customs practice, at an annual stipend of $25,000, better than any civil servant received at that time. The company showed its respect for him by providing him with a New York apartment, enabling him to keep his home in Washington. They also took over the unpublished manuscript of *Tariff Classification,* and the government lost it.

For many years after his retirement, Johnson still enjoyed the respect and affection of Customs personnel. One of his most ardent admirers, who must remain nameless, writes: ". . . It is apparent that the law has given better awards to many who had less of what it takes. In Johnson's case, but for one impulsive error, there is no way to guess where his career might have stopped."

His memorable book *Johnson on Tariff Classification,* encyclopedic in scope and detail, set the Customs Service on its path toward modernization, with its simplified definitions of the involved tariff laws. He introduced the job of budget control officer and fathered legislative proposals many of which made life simpler for the American trading and traveling community. He started a trend which was to continue for years, and which still hasn't ended.

Ralph Kelly was the next permanent commissioner of Customs after Frank Dow.

Ralph Kelly, U.S. Commissioner of Customs
from 1954 to 1961.

He served as commissioner from 1954 to 1961 and was an appointee of Treasury Secretary George M. Humphrey. Kelly was born in Boston in 1888, earned his engineering degree at Harvard, and in 1909, at the age of twenty-one, took his first job as a junior engineer in the East Pittsburgh plant of the Westinghouse Electric Corporation. During World War I, he served for two years as a navy lieutenant, later returning to Westinghouse. He rose through the ranks and was appointed vice president in charge of sales in 1938. In 1942 he was appointed executive vice president and director of the Baldwin Locomotive Works at Eddystone, Pennsylvania, finally becoming president. He relinquished his business responsibilities upon his appointment as commissioner.

The simplification of the complex customs procedures that had started during the incumbency of Frank Dow received new impetus during Kelly's administration. Working in close coordination with private industry in the fields of commercial trading and travel, Customs and Treasury planners succeeded in winning Congressional support for the Customs Simplification Acts of 1953, 1954, and 1956, all enacted after protracted debate.

Behind these efforts at reform and modernization was the conviction that the Customs Service had to bring its procedures into modern focus if it was to cope with sharply rising foreign trade and international travel. Customs collections neared the billion dollar mark in 1956—$983 million. Formal entries increased 10.8 percent over the previous calendar year to well over the million mark. During that same year about 129,000,000 people crossed the borders of the U.S., while the number of carriers entering the country rose by 11 percent. Invoices for goods increased 6.2 percent.

The striking thing about these figures is the fact that the staff of the Customs Service actually *dropped* by approximately 17 percent during the same period— the result of the planning of Assistant Secretary of the Treasury H. Chapman Rose and his technical assistant Clark Winter, later vice president of the American Express Company.

The American people, and specifically the commercial importers and the traveling public, were the principal beneficiaries of the passage of the Simplification Acts, which repealed many of the archaic laws and practices that had been on the books for a century and a half.

The 1953 Act, for example, eliminated the requirement that every calculation of customs duty be verified by comptrollers of Customs. This reduced the tremen-

In a stepped-up effort to expose frauds against the Treasury, special import control teams have been established, consisting of an inspector, an import specialist, and a special agent, to perform random spot checks on imported goods. In these pictures, members of these special teams examine recently imported foreign cars and heavy machinery.

dous backlog of merchandise entries awaiting final determination of their duty and tax status, officially described as "liquidation." At the time this bill was enacted, the backlog had reached four hundred thousand merchandise entries awaiting liquidation. It required three and a half years to cut down that mountain of unfinished business by approximately 50 percent. It doesn't take an expert to realize what this meant to a businessman who had to wait years to find out how much customs duty he owed the government before placing his goods for sale in the marketplace.

Another provision of the Simplification Act eliminated many petty, harassing regulations. It eliminated the requirement that the great majority of commercial importations had to have invoices certified by a United States Consulate in the country of origin. Another important improvement permitted corrections of purely clerical-type errors in duty computations without court action, a provision that had plagued importers for years. The process of liquidation, so important in the customs process, was thereby speeded up.

The Act also facilitated international travel, especially between the United States and Canada and between the United States and Mexico. Previously, U.S. residents visiting Canada and returning to the United States within forty-eight hours were allowed only one dollar's worth of merchandise free of duty. This was increased to the more realistic figure of ten dollars. Tourists from Canada and Mexico visiting the U.S.A. in their private automobiles no longer had to register their cars when they crossed the border. New procedures made it possible for tourist purchases admitted free of duty to be returned for repair or exchange, without resorting to baffling and frustrating Customs procedures.

New legislation in 1954 was designed to put in motion a series of studies making the tariff laws more comprehensible and enforceable. Parts of the tariff law were unbelievably contradictory and confusing. For example, imported false teeth had been classified in the category of chinaware! Procedures were set up enabling importers to obtain a "firm" classification of their merchandise, prior to its importation, by providing samples and descriptive information.

The Customs procedures were refined and honed further yet in another Simplification Act in 1956, based on intensive studies by special valuation task forces, groups of technical experts who were brought to the Customs Service from all over the country to work on the project.

Customs worked with airlines, steamship companies, and travel agencies in devising new concepts for facilitating the greatly increased volume of passengers arriving from overseas by sea and air. A modified baggage declaration form, which eliminated the legalistic, involved language often found in government issuances, was devised. A new "supermarket" system was developed for persons arriving by plane, speeding up unloading and Customs examinations.

"There will be no letup on the search for further economies and improvements," said Commissioner Kelly. "The economic well-being of the United States and that of the entire free world is dependent to a very large extent on a healthy international trade. It is our policy to remove as many obstacles to trade as possible, while providing adequate protection to the American people and business."

The concept of public service as being central to the mission of the Customs Service didn't find full expression in policies and programs until the administration of Commissioner of Customs, later Court of Claims Judge, Philip Nichols, Jr., who served from 1961 to 1964. His administration was a radical change from that of his predecessors, who felt that the Customs officer's job was simply to protect the Treasury against fraud and to collect the revenues due under the tariff laws of the United States.

Philip Nichols, Jr., U.S. Commissioner of Customs from 1961 to 1964. In 1964 Nichols was made a judge of the U.S. Customs Court.

The Nichols formula focused on the importance of courtesy and accommodation, without sacrificing professionalism and enforcement. The son of a Massachusetts circuit court judge, Nichols had been with the Treasury Department from 1946 to 1951 as an assistant general counsel for Customs and Narcotics. He was chairman of a committee that drafted legislation to simplify Customs laws and procedures, and was very conversant with the intricacies of the Tariff Act.

He had served with the Lands Division of the Justice Department, the War Production Board, and the Renegotiation Board. During World War II he was a U.S. Navy commander. Coupled with his extensive expertise in various areas was a keen sense of humor, an insatiable appetite to gather facts, and a love of people and travel. He was not a man who would defy bureaucratic roadblocks in a headlong flight from the shackles of historic precedent. Rather, he kept faith with his background as a career civil servant and chose the slow road to reform, but without faltering in direction and purpose.

In recent years Customs has tried to change
its public image, to put increasing emphasis
on courtesy as part of the inspection procedure, and through special exhibits such as
these explain to Americans how the service
protects the nation and why seemingly
harassing rules and regulations are
necessary.

When Nichols was sworn in as commissioner by Secretary of the Treasury Douglas Dillon on March 24, 1961, the Bureau of Customs was in its 172nd year. The previous year it had collected $2 billion in revenue with a budget of $73 million. It had about 8,600 employees thinly deployed among 286 ports of entry, and it was top-heavy with 53 presidential appointees in supervisory positions, some of whom knew little or nothing about Customs, and admitted it. The political mold within which the agency was forced to carry out its nonpolitical functions impeded modernization planning.

Commissioner Nichols found himself at the helm of a vast, sprawling, fragmented agency, spread out along the east and west coasts, and throughout the interior—an organization that was sorely in need of consolidation and a greater awareness of its responsibilities to the public. Many of its procedures and its philosophy had their origin in eighteenth-century practices that had been adopted in their identical form from England. Indeed, a British customs officer of 1762 would have had relatively little trouble adapting himself to U.S. Customs practices in 1962—two centuries later.

The long-range program put into effect by Commissioner Nichols was based upon an in-depth study made at the beginning of his administration. It was commonly known as the O'Connell Report, named for the chairman of the study group.

Joseph J. O'Connell was a distinguished Washington attorney and noted transportation authority, who for many years had represented international airlines and travel organizations. The mission of his committee, which included Treasury, Customs, and Bureau of the Budget members, was deceptively simple: to study means of speeding up and streamlining the clearance of baggage and passengers entering the United States.

The O'Connell Report, following lengthy research, testing, and study in many countries in addition to the United States, was submitted to Treasury Secretary Douglas Dillon in January 1962. Its far-reaching recommendations set the course for Customs procedures and policies for years to come. They provided Commissioner Nichols and his successors with a blueprint for the reconstruction of the Customs Service in keeping with twentieth-century concepts of management, training, recruitment, the processing of passengers and merchandise, and public service and public relations. Later reorganizations were built upon the foundation laid by the O'Connell study.

The O'Connell Committee's mission was to determine whether existing procedures "discouraged" foreign tourists from visiting the United States, which was, for the first time in history, seeking to lure them to this country. It also sought to determine whether U.S. Customs was regarded as a "harassment" and, if so, what could be done about it. Behind this apparently simple frame of reference was the need for drastic changes in policy, the need for a restatement of purpose; in short, the need for an action program to meet the challenges of the age of technology. "Customs is an old service," the Task Force report observed, "but it must live in a world made new by radical change, not only in transportation, but also in living standards, communications technology, politics, and international trade. The prospect of change is not a new one, but at this juncture we must face up not just to change but to change at an ever-increasing pace."

While acknowledging the "generally effective and responsive" job being done by Customs, the report dealt with the important new role the agency now had to play in America's international affairs. Additional resources would be needed, and personnel "must, by temperament, training, and sincere recognition of the significance of their actions, be able and willing to carry out the mission."

The historic dual mission of the Customs Service, responsibility for collection of revenue and enforcement of the law, was carried out by levying duties on imported merchandise, and by the detection and prevention of attempts to evade the payment of these duties, and the interdiction of articles introduced into the United States that were prohibited or restricted by Customs laws, regulations, and quotas, or by the laws of other government agencies. What was the best way of carrying out these responsibilities in the world's most highly industrialized economy? How could a federal agency make the maximum use of its limited resources in light of the explosions in population, travel, and world trade?

The search for new approaches was intensified by the publication of the O'Connell report. Little importance had been attached by Customs to public opinion concerning America; foreign tourist promotion was left to shipping companies and the airlines, to a handful of cities and states, and to the travel agencies. So far as Customs was concerned, its inspectors were expected to be law enforcers, with little or no regard for the feelings of the passengers whose baggage they examined. But America's policy-makers were increasingly aware that, in its role as leader of the free world, the United States was expected to show that it respected other nationalities and ethnic groups and their rights as human beings. The idea had also taken hold that foreign visitors to the U.S.A. could have a decisive influence on public opinion and ultimately play a part in influencing the leadership of their own countries.

In the area of tourist development, the Customs officers functioning at ports of entry were a significant factor in encouraging visitors or influencing them to keep away. The tourist boom in other countries produced important sources of income, and this was noted in the Congress and the White House.

Travelers encounter several border control agencies upon entering the U.S.A. For the foreign tourist, the efficiency and courtesy of Customs officers reflect the attitude of the United States government and the American people toward him, toward his nation, and his particular ethnic group. Racism, discourtesy, and suspicion severely discouraged visitors who came from distant shores at great expense to see the America they had heard so much about. The same feelings of fear and ignorance of Customs were characteristic not only of foreign visitors but returning Americans as well.

The dilemma in which Customs inspectors find themselves was based first upon the expectation that they would perform as effective enforcers of the laws governing admission to the United States, while at the same time playing the part of goodwill ambassadors. Their job is to prevent smuggling—the smuggling of drugs and high-tariff items such as jewelry, watch movements, and a wide range of other dutiable goods that are often brought into the country illegally.

Department of Agriculture regulations prohibit or restrict the importation of

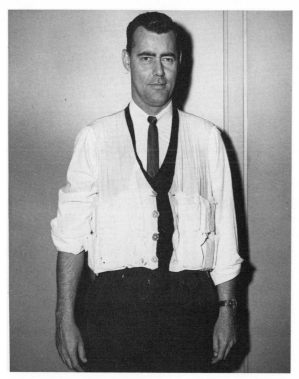

A Customs inspector demonstrates how these small gold bars were smuggled into the country in a vest.

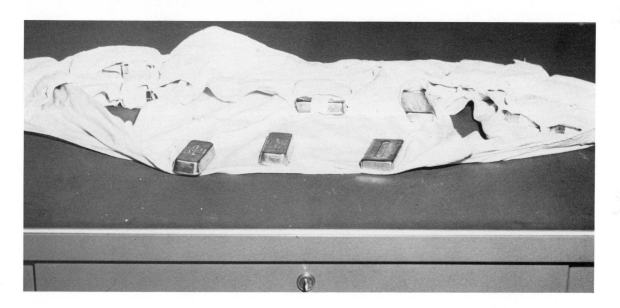

domestic animals, plants, and their products, that is, meats, fruits, vegetables, seeds, and so on. This is done to protect our agriculture against foreign insect pests and diseases. The Public Health Service controls the importation of dogs, cats, monkeys, and psittacine birds, such as parrots and parakeets, as a means of controlling the spread of diseases like rabies, yellow fever, and psittacosis, or "parrot fever." The Food and Drug Administration bars the importation of candy containing any alcohol or nonnutritive substances, because such candy is often adulterated.

Parrots like the ones shown here, seized at
the Mexican border, are a prohibited import
because they are disease carriers and may
spread this disease to certain species of
poultry.

The Fish and Wildlife Service prohibits or restricts the importation of wild
animals and birds, their dead bodies, and their plumage and eggs. The Foreign
Assets Control office prohibits imports of any kind from Rhodesia, North Korea,
North Vietnam, and Cuba. This Treasury Department agency requires import
licenses or certificates of origin for goods which have been located in Hong Kong,
Macao, or any Soviet bloc country, if such articles were produced or manufactured in Communist China or North Korea or any of the other countries covered
by the economic boycott policies of the United States.

Customs is responsible for ensuring that all these laws and regulations are
enforced. The service thus rendered is done on a reimbursable basis. Thus, the
Department of Agriculture reimburses Customs annually for this work. The
department maintains a small force of its own at the larger ports of entry such as
New York, but at most of the three hundred other ports of entry throughout the
country, Customs does the job.

Customs trains its personnel in these and many other statutes for close to forty
federal agencies, such as the Atomic Energy Commission, the Coast Guard, the
Defense Department, and others. It even enforces the laws of a number of individual states that limit the amount of alcoholic beverages which may be brought
into a state by an arrival from abroad.

Baggage inspection is the best-known function performed by Customs in most
countries. The authority for searching the effects of persons entering the United
States without a warrant was established by the first Congress on March 2, 1789. It
was reaffirmed in sections 467, 496, and 582 of the Tariff Act of 1930, and in
section 23.1(3) of Customs Regulations. Down through the centuries, this author-

ity has been challenged as being in violation of the Fourth Amendment to the Constitution, which provides that "the right of the people to be secure in their persons, houses, papers, and effects, against unreasonable searches and seizures, shall not be violated."

However, the Supreme Court has ruled, and it is now well established, that Customs Officers may search the baggage of persons entering the United States without a search warrant and may seize articles found to be illegally imported.

The number of persons processed in one year through Customs prior to entering the U.S. has skyrocketed to astronomical proportions. At this time of writing, their numbers exceed 265 million, more than our entire population.

Passengers cross the vast 30,000-mile borders of the United States and its possessions, in automobiles, planes, and boats. Many thousands walk back and forth across the U.S.–Mexican border, working on one side and living on the other. At San Ysidro, California, alone, for instance, more than eight million vehicles and twenty-eight million persons are clocked in by Customs each year. Every one of these individuals must be cleared through Customs; every one presents a challenge; many have special problems which consume considerable time and effort.

Exacerbating the overall problem was the policy of trying to open every piece of baggage, as unrealistic an instruction as could be imagined, but this was the regulation. Sometimes it was carried out and sometimes it was not. Later, it was replaced by the more practical and realistic primary and secondary system, which was a kind of screening system designed to speed through Customs the innocent traveler, and isolate those calling for more attentive examination.

The Customs station at San Ysidro, California, near the Mexican border, on a typical Sunday afternoon. The volume of automobile traffic at land border crossings has increased dramatically in the last decade, putting a very great strain on Customs personnel, particularly during the period when the detection and interdiction of drug smugglers was the service's first priority.

A passenger attempted to smuggle in this mongoose in a piece of hand luggage. The importation of the mongoose is prohibited because of its ferocious attacks on native wildlife and its prolific breeding habits.

A rather unexpected seizure for Customs officials, a young orang-utan, discovered at Dulles Airport. Customs cooperates with many countries to protect wildlife, and this creature was seized in order to determine whether or not he had been captured and illegally exported from his homeland.

Another troublesome arrival for Customs inspectors, one of two one-ton rhinos that were shipped to the San Diego Zoo from South Africa. The animals had to be shipped in crates facing each other to prevent them from going on the rampage during transit. Courtesy of the Port of Mobile.

Here Customs inspectors remove bricks of
marihuana from special sheet metal shelves
welded to the underside of a smuggler's
automobile.

The intensity of the inspection of passengers and their baggage varies with circumstances. The volume of traffic, the type of smuggling currently in vogue, the amount and type of baggage being carried, the length of one's stay abroad, the places visited; all are considered by the Customs officer.

Passengers arriving from overseas some years ago could anticipate that all or most of their baggage would be opened and inspected, in keeping with United States Department of Agriculture statutes barring insect pests and diseases injurious to domestic plants and livestock. During peak periods of travel at congested airports such as John F. Kennedy Airport in New York, when Customs personnel were spread thin, a system of spot-checking overseas baggage was instituted to avoid unreasonable delays. The 100 percent inspection policy was reinstated in these cases as soon as the peak periods had passed.

At the larger land border crossing points, there are primary and secondary inspection areas. Officers at the primary screening points decide, on the basis of answers to a few brief questions and a cursory inspection of a vehicle, whether the arrivals can be cleared immediately, or whether they must be referred to the secondary area for further interrogation, inspection, or payment of customs duties. The cursory inspection usually involves careful scrutiny of the interior, the glove compartment, or the trunk. During the war on drugs in the seventies, vehicle examination was to become far more painstaking and thorough. Ingenious drug smugglers often concealed their cargo in automobile tires, behind hubcaps, in false-bottomed trunks, and even in phony gas tanks.

At the smaller one-man points of entry along the Canadian and Mexican borders, there are no secondary inspection areas. The same inspection policy is followed, except that the officer on duty performs both primary and secondary examinations. If it becomes necessary to take an arrival into the office to make out a customs declaration, traffic must wait until the officer completes his paper work. However, traffic at the smaller crossing points is generally light enough to permit the officer to perform his secondary examinations without delaying passengers and vehicles beyond a reasonable time. A dual inspection procedure is in effect in some of these places, enabling Customs and Immigration inspectors to perform each other's duties. At larger entry points, a Customs or an Immigration officer does the preliminary screening for both services, referring arrivals when necessary to either the Customs or Immigration secondary areas.

The traffic jams and delays at jumbo-size ports of entry such as New York's John F. Kennedy Airport derive from the rate of aircraft arrivals during the mornings and late afternoon hours. Peak loads occur daily, weekly, and seasonally, and there are peak loads within peak loads. When personnel are assigned to the inspection lanes during high intensity periods, there is the problem of keeping them busy during the intervening slack periods. At John F. Kennedy Airport, the peak-load problem was partially solved by designating a certain number of inspectors as inspector-liquidators. Liquidation in Customs parlance consists of the "mopping-up" phase of the entire process of clearance and assessment of duties on imported merchandise. The function of the liquidator is to fix the rate of duty and make the computations necessary to determine the final amount of duty. In other areas, inspectors are borrowed from cargo work and detailed to passenger lanes, but this delays cargo examination.

Out of the total of thirty-three recommendations for reform and modernization in the O'Connell report, all but five were approved by the Treasury-Customs Steering Committee, and were given to Commissioner Nichols and his staff to put into effect.

The new Customs National Training Center
at Hofstra University on Long Island.

In the twentieth century the Customs inspector or special agent has had to become a truly professional law enforcement officer, and training programs have come to involve everything from classwork to physical self-defense, from arrest-and-search procedures required for dangerous criminals to proficiency with firearms.

New performance evaluation standards were urged for the selection of inspectors; new training methods and refresher courses were suggested; and the establishment of a Customs Training Academy was proposed. The committee emphasized the importance of a foreign language capability for baggage inspectors. Employee associations were invited to participate in formulating training courses "geared to increasing the knowledge and stature" of the inspection forces.

The Task Force recommended that incentive awards, including medals, certificates, within-grade promotions, and public recognition, be introduced as morale builders and as a means of increasing effectiveness and productivity. Coupled with this was the suggestion that sanctions be applied to employees who did not measure up to the new standards.

The Bureau of Customs was urged to prepare a code of minimum standards for passenger facilities at terminals where it operated—a critically needed reform, especially in such ports of entry as New York, where obsolete and unsightly piers imposed hardships on passengers and Customs inspectors alike. Arriving passengers, unaware of the fact that these piers, some of them half a century old, were under the control of the cities in which they were located, freely blamed Customs for the conditions which they found upon returning home after experiencing the plush, comfortable conditions prevailing at European points of departure. Many of these European ports had been reconstructed and modernized, with U.S. financial aid, after being subjected to bombing in World War II. Commissioner Nichols once remarked: "Apparently it takes a bombing attack to bring Port Authorities to the realization that piers have to be rebuilt."

Some of the O'Connell Committee recommendations dealt more directly with basic Customs facilities, and called for the substitution of an "oral" for a written baggage declaration when the value of items acquired abroad was less than the allowable exemption; the elimination of the "to follow" provision, under which items coming into the United States by mail were included in the $100 exemption allowed returning U.S. residents; legislation imposing a flat 10 percent rate of duty on all tourist imports, and the introduction of a system of coordinated screening operations by Customs, Immigration, Public Health, and Agriculture agencies.

The millions of persons who arrive at U.S. ports of entry in the decade of the seventies take for granted many of these reforms. But they required a great deal of effort, study, and experimentation before they could be taken off the drawing boards and put into effect. The recommendation for a flat rate of duty, a concept which prevails in most areas of the world, still has never won Congressional sanction. Some progress has been made in rejuvenating the piers of New York, but arrivals on United States-bound transoceanic ships are still shocked by the miserable conditions along New York's famous waterfront.

Nichols's successor, Lester D. Johnson, perpetuated the tradition out of the personal conviction that the nebulous word "public" translated into people who were also consumers and that consumers had rights, and insisted upon them. Among these were the right to courtesy, an explanation of the law, and the maximum freedom from travel restrictions within the context of that law.

Lester D. Johnson brought to bear on his new job more than three decades of varied and extensive experience in Customs. He had started as a messenger and clerk in San Francisco, worked as an appraiser and as a Customs representative in the Far East and in Europe, and was chief of the Office of Investigations at Bureau Headquarters for years. Thus his expertise was complete and total, virtually unmatched in any commissioner before or since. Not only did Johnson know Customs, but he had also mastered several European languages, as well as Japanese. Absolute integrity and stability in his administrative craftsmanship were his most striking characteristics. His photographic memory for facts, names, places, case histories, and details gave Lester Johnson his widely acknowledged reputation as a "walking encyclopedia."

Johnson worked quietly and efficiently at the frustrating task of "running fast in order to stand still." The rising Customs work load in terms of air travelers and the volume of cargo requiring customs clearance were mounting with relentless momentum. But appropriations for the Customs Service lagged far behind. It was difficult to believe that an agency which produced more than $23 in revenue for each single dollar it received for operations would be left by economy-minded Congressional committees to scrape and scrimp and "make do" with an enrolled personnel strength that was smaller than the number of Customs employees in the time of Calvin Coolidge—less than Canadian Customs, less than the Customs strength of the United Kingdom, West Germany, France, or even the Low Countries together. Johnson presented his case skillfully before Appropriations Committee after Appropriations Committee, but to no avail.

Not until Johnson's successor came aboard, and the drug problem was recognized as a national epidemic, did the Customs Service finally receive a significant increase in funds and personnel. This was no reflection on Lester Johnson's skill and ability as an administrator, but it required the realization that addiction to dangerous drugs, such as heroin and cocaine, was no longer confined to America's ghettoes but was now to be found in cities and towns throughout the nation, in high schools and colleges, in homes and on the streets. The grand awakening came in 1969 and 1970, and Congress gave the Customs Service the funding and personnel it needed to perform its role and carry out its responsibility as America's "first line of defense" in the war against narcotics.

Myles J. Ambrose, who became Commissioner in 1969, had been a special assistant to the secretary of the treasury during the Eisenhower Administration, during which time he acquired a familiarity with Customs and other enforcement agencies. He had served as Waterfront Commissioner in New York City, and was a dynamic, hard-driving person who inspired loyalty as well as hard work among those who served under him.

Ambrose succeeded in winning over not only congressional committees but the White House itself in his relentless drive for support of a larger, more effective Customs enforcement system. For example, he would invite a group of congressmen or senators to accompany him on a field trip to a "hot spot," where smugglers were being nabbed by the hundreds, and there Ambrose would dazzle his guests with an avalanche of statistics and exhibits.

Myles J. Ambrose, Commissioner of Customs
from 1969 to 1972.

Vernon D. Acree, the present U.S.
Commissioner of Customs.

With the assistance of a remarkable deputy, Edwin F. Rains, an attorney with thirty-five years of experience in Customs and Treasury legal work, Ambrose was able to concentrate his attention on the drug war. Leaving the complex task of handling Customs' technical problems to Rains, Commissioner Ambrose fought for and received from Congress substantial supplemental appropriations. He used the funds to build up Customs technology in order to give muscle to the enforcement staff. The number of Customs agents in investigative work steadily grew. Their seizures and arrests mounted wildly. Their morale and their productivity had never been so high. It was only a matter of time before the public would begin to appreciate the job Customs was doing. All the media, printed and electronic, began to take notice. The White House asked Ambrose to give demonstrations and exhibits for newsmen, for selected editors and television commentators, for the clergy, and other special groups invited to Washington for the purpose.

It came as no surprise when the President invited Ambrose to accept an appointment as his special adviser on narcotic drugs and, concurrently, as special assistant attorney general in charge of the Justice Department's antinarcotic drug program.

Did the years of effort and the expenditure of tens of millions on the drug war have the desired effect? Only time will tell. At the time of writing, both the U.S. Customs Service and the Drug Enforcement Administration are still waging an ongoing battle against international traffickers; still making enormous seizures and arrests; still stalking the smugglers and the peddlers, domestic and foreign. There has been a drop in heroin coming into the U.S., but there are signs that a new generation of smugglers will soon appear. Perhaps the war will never be really won. Perhaps it is up to the parents and teachers of America to do the job in the homes and schoolrooms, rather than to Customs men to do it on the borders.

The massive effort to halt the spread of airplane hijacking, which was assigned to the U.S. Customs Service, also did little to advance the "forgotten cause of the international passenger," in the words of one travel writer. But the menace to Americans of both narcotic drugs and air piracy admittedly demanded unprecedented measures.

New initiatives introduced by Vernon D. Acree, the twenty-first commissioner, appointed by the then Secretary of the Treasury John Connally, in 1972, marked another turning point in the history of Customs. At age fifty-three, Acree brought to bear on the task of streamlining and modernizing the Customs Service a thirty-year career of experience and expertise as a criminal investigator and an administrator. He developed a balanced enforcement program in which every individual part of the service supports and complements the other, building morale and esprit de corps, as well as the capacity for coping with the increased demands placed upon Customs by the relentless growth and expansion of international trade and travel.

In recognition of his ability Acree received a prestigious Rockefeller Public Service award of $10,000 for his work while serving as assistant commissioner of the Internal Revenue Service prior to his appointment to Customs. Although eligible for retirement after thirty-six years of federal service, Acree accepted the assignment out of a deep personal commitment to public service, and because of the challenge posed by an incredibly complex job.

There is little doubt that the U.S. Customs Service needed Acree's perspectives and experience; his record after two years in office justified the former Treasury Secretary's judgment.

"This has been a year of significant accomplishment and change within the Customs Service," Commissioner Acree told a House Subcommittee on Appropriations in April 1974, "none the least of which was our change in name."

The change to which he was referring bespoke his deep-seated conviction that the old Bureau of Customs, now officially the U.S. Customs Service, needed to project to the American people an image not of a bureaucracy, shackled with outworn and obsolete procedures and attitudes, but of a youthful, vigorous, and forward-looking agency, dedicated to serving the country.

Much of this change resulted from the transfer, in July 1973, of crack Customs narcotic investigators, intelligence functionaries, and related personnel and resources to a new entity in the Justice Department called the Drug Enforcement Administration. The transfer required a major overhaul of structure and functions to determine what would be the most effective way of using the remaining enforcement manpower in Customs.

As a result of this review, the field structure of the Office of Investigations was made to conform to the nine regular Customs Regions into which the country was divided. Seventeen foreign offices and eighteen domestic offices were abolished, in order to promote a more uniform and efficient approach to a wide range of investigative activities, from commercial fraud to global terrorism.

Customs patrol operations along the borders, between ports of entry, at piers and airports from coast to coast, were reinstated, twenty-five years after the legendary Customs Border Patrol had been abolished by Commissioner W. R. Johnson in 1948. The restored Customs Patrol had spectacular results in terms of arrests of smugglers and seizures of every conceivable kind of contraband. Air and marine support activities were realigned in order to effect a consolidation of all uniformed enforcement personnel, as a means of strengthening and sharpening the agency's ability to interdict and apprehend violators of the law.

Acree ordered the consolidation of "support" functions such as the highly sophisticated "Treasury Enforcement Communications System" (popularly referred to as TECS) with Customs communications and research activities in a new headquarters organization, the Office of Enforcement Support. Tactical interdiction units, fully equipped with sophisticated communications apparatus, were placed in strategic locations around the entire perimeter of the United States, and plans were made to expand into other areas.

The Office of Investigations, until 1972, was heavily involved in narcotics-related investigations because of overriding national priorities. The formation of the Drug Enforcement Administration enabled Acree to put new emphasis on the full range of other Customs investigatory responsibilities that had been almost forgotten in the drug interdiction effort. During the period from July 1973 to April 1974, Customs special agents made tremendous strides in the recovery of illegally

This nearly extinct bird, originally from
China or possibly India, was seized in a New
York City mail room. It was smuggled in
so that its rare feathers might be used in
making fishing flies.

imported art and artifacts; in the mass arrest of commercial parrot smugglers; in
making large seizures of gold and silver coins; in prosecuting major neutrality
violation cases and major fraud conspiracies. These areas of traditional Customs
operations had been long overshadowed by the all-consuming fight on narcotics.

Originally, the Customs Division was divided into three main units: the office of the chief counsel; the administrative unit, and the Customs agency service. Field operations were directed from the Washington office, which adjudicated legal and administrative problems based on its interpretation of the Tariff Act, related laws, and Customs regulations. The Agency service, now called the office of investigations, included the Treasury-Customs representatives abroad, as well as a force of intensively trained agents who investigated fraud on the government, undervaluation, and a wide range of other problems.

Before the reorganization of 1973, the top priority mission of the Office of Investigations was to stop the smuggling of narcotics. Under the reorganization, Customs sustained the loss of 500 of its crack agents, another 250 or so support personnel, a large portion of its equipment, including boats, sensors, and communications devices, and considerable funds, all transferred to the Drug Enforcement Administration of the Justice Department. But, true to its tradition, the Customs Service bounced back, recovering through Congressional appropriations much of what it had lost, thanks to the tenacity and determination of its present commissioner, Vernon D. Acree, who declared he had not taken the job to "preside over the dismemberment of Customs." In fact, during the year and a half following the reorganization, Customs broke all previous records for seizing drugs along the Mexican border at and between ports of entry. The service realigned its priorities, renewed its crackdown on commercial fraud cases and related violations, dug in to cope with an ever-increasing work load in travel and trade, and continued to pursue its mission with conviction, high esprit de corps, and a dedication to duty unmatched in any other governmental agency.

The central thrust of the Reorganization Act of 1973 was to transfer the investigation of drug cases to the Justice Department. But it must be emphasized again that this did not relieve U.S. Customs of one of its basic functions, the interdiction of narcotics *at* and *between* ports of entry. Nor did it alter in any way the traditional role of Customs as the nation's border guard and protector of the Treasury.

	Estimated Completed Cases	Share of Work Load
Technical Investigations (Fraud and Undervaluation)	8,250	33%
Smuggling and Organized Crime Investigations	5,500	22%
Regulatory Investigations (Licenses, marking, currency violations, prohibited imports, etc.)	5,000	20%
Special, Verification, and Foreign Investigations	6,250	25%
TOTAL	25,000	100%

When the oil-producing states of the Middle East imposed an embargo on oil exports to the United States in 1974 and the public became conscious of the energy crisis, Customs was given the responsibility of keeping accurate statistical data on the availability of foreign oil. Here Customs inspectors climb a fuel storage tank in Norfolk, Virginia, to check on the volume of oil shipped to the refinery.

A group of Mercedes Benz automobiles are driven off the Swedish freighter *Atlantic Span*. Since 1968, the Customs Service has had the additional responsibility of ensuring that all foreign cars brought into the country meet federal safety and air pollution requirements. For dockside Customs personnel, this has meant more paper work and actual spot checks of the vehicles.

In 1974, another responsibility was given to the Customs Service: to provide manpower and other resources to assist in meeting the country's energy crisis by helping the new Federal Energy Office with staffing, administrative help, recruitment, and most important, by reporting vital daily oil import information. Thus, once again, the Customs Service was called upon, as had happened so many times before in United States history, to come to its country's rescue in a crisis.

International Programs

The growing narcotic and dangerous drug epidemic in the United States prompted President Nixon in 1971 to establish the Cabinet Committee on International Narcotics Control (CCINC). Its mission was to consider programs and

Customs also conducts training programs for the employees of foreign Customs services. Here a United States AID official presents graduation certificates to a group of officers of the Laotian Customs Service.

Ghanaian and Jordanian Customs officials
participate in a seminar as part of the
Foreign Customs Assistance Enforcement
Program.

activities designed to stimulate greater awareness and interest on the part of the
world community in the narcotics problem and to suggest means of bringing it
under control.

   Although narcotics investigative activities were now the responsibility of the
Drug Enforcement Administration, Customs was still America's kingpin in border
interdiction and liaison with other Customs services of the world. The U.S. Customs training program was geared to demonstrate to foreign enforcement officials
modern American methods of border surveillance and control, interdiction techniques, antismuggling programs, cargo control, and search-and-seizure procedures. A real impact was made on many countries, and in less than a year Customs had trained more than a thousand foreign Customs officers and executives
from twenty-seven different countries. The value of this program is evident in the
increasing rate of drug seizures in those countries; every seizure abroad meant
that much lessening of the supply that could conceivably end up on American
streets.

Nearly every country requested additional training. Through these mutual assistance and training programs, the U.S. Customs Service has been able to stimulate better communications with other nations, several of which were able to increase their national revenues, thereby reducing their dependence upon foreign aid, much of it American in origin. Customs provided training for twenty-one of the fifty-three countries on the original CCINC priority list, and plans to train the personnel of the remaining thirty-two countries in 1975 and 1976.

Customs efforts in support of the CCINC have also been improved by its increasingly active participation in the Customs Cooperation Council (CCC), an international information exchange representing eighty-seven participating countries. The CCC has played a major role in simplifying Customs procedures throughout the world, and it is playing an increasing role in worldwide antismuggling and antifraud programs. In October 1973, the U.S. Customs Service hosted the tenth annual meeting of the Customs investigative services of fifty-four of the member nations. The meeting produced machinery for a continuing exchange of information on international smuggling, as well as new investigative techniques to detect fraud and other violations.

The U.S. Customs Service has nine operating foreign offices which are actively expanding their contacts with foreign customs and police officials, representatives of business and industry, and the general public. These contacts produce countless investigative leads, which are then funneled to U.S. Customs domestic field offices. The foreign offices are primarily responsible for a wide variety of cases against corporations, large and small, some of them involving tens of millions of dollars in penalties levied against them for attempting to defraud the treasury. These foreign operations are actively supported by a senior special agent assigned as liaison officer to the U.S. National Central Bureau of Interpol in Washington. The objective is to make Interpol a two-way street for the exchange of international smuggling intelligence and the coordination of major international investigations.

The New Duty Assessment System

To modernize its procedures to cope with America's ever-expanding trade, Customs has changed its policy to insure compliance with the new Customs duty assessment system.

Termed "compliance by selectivity," the new policy moves away from the notion that in order to secure compliance, Customs has to physically examine and individually process each and every importation into the United States. In lieu of this, the agency is concentrating its limited resources on the high-payoff, high-risk transactions, depending largely on importers and international carriers themselves to comply voluntarily with Customs requirements, subject to spot checks and audits.

The key element in the success of this program of modernization is the development of an "external audit" capability, in order to be selective in identifying those areas requiring a concentrated effort. This capability would permit Customs to audit the accounts and records of importers, carriers, and others doing business with Customs on a selective basis, to insure the reliability of this compliance system.

The principal areas for external audit include merchandise from insular possessions, American goods assembled abroad, drawback claims, goods covered under the Automotive Products Trade Act, duty-free-shop purchases, and other products which are conditionally free of duty. There has also been developed a system for handling a major portion of the import work load on an account basis. Duty Assessment By Account (DABA) is a major effort to modernize the way Customs does business with the commercial importing community. Under this system major importers account for their importations on a periodic basis rather than by individual transactions for each importation.

"The Customs Service is a major revenue-producing branch of our government," stated Commissioner Acree, "collecting substantial sums of money for the government's operation at a very low cost, providing essential enforcement support to high priority programs. Our work load continues to rise sharply and some of the lines go practically off the charts. They contrast vividly with the much slower rate of growth for manpower. The total manpower of the U.S. Customs Service is less than the size of some municipal police forces and is much smaller than most European Customs services."

The Air Security Program

Under an agreement between the Department of the Treasury and the Department of Transportation, established on October 28, 1970, the U.S. Customs Service pro-

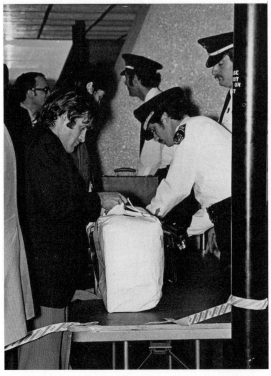

For a time Customs personnel also served as "sky marshals" in a nationwide effort to eliminate airline hijacking. Here Customs security officers at Dulles International Airport in Washington, D.C., examine passenger baggage prior to departure.

vided "predeparture inspection" and screening on the ground, and in-flight protection for American flag airline carriers.

In 1973, the federal program was ordered terminated and new civil aviation security measures now require airport operators to provide their own law enforcement officers to support airline security requirements. Customs was able to reduce its air security efforts in 1972–73 from a total of one thousand three hundred air security officers to a total of sixty. Most of these trained and dedicated Customs security officers were transferred to other positions to meet high priority enforcement needs. Within this short period the record of the Customs Service in this area was a remarkable one. Not a single plane whose passengers had been screened by a Customs security officer was ever hijacked in the U.S.A. These security officers made 3,828 arrests, some in-flight; seized 2,836 weapons; made 248 seizures of hard drugs and 1,667 seizures of marihuana and other dangerous drugs. This program provided a remarkable example of professional federal law enforcement responsiveness to a critically dangerous situation, and illustrated once more the versatility and dedication of the U.S. Customs Service. It was largely unnoticed in the media and, to this day, remains almost unknown to the American people.

The Air Support Program

The U.S. Customs in 1974 had the country's only completely operational air support system concerned with interdicting smuggling by aircraft and with supporting Customs ground and sea enforcement operations. The program makes use of high performance aircraft, light spotter aircraft, helicopters, forward-looking infrared sensors (FLIRS), airborne and mobile ground radar, a sophisticated communications network, and other tracking and detection equipment. These are essential in this era of the sophisticated professional smuggler who, because of the high profits involved, is able to employ the most modern aircraft available and the same sophisticated hardware. This equipment gives to Customs unique air surveillance capabilities, which are used not only for the independent interdiction of air smuggling but for the support of related law enforcement activities by other federal, state, and local jurisdictions.

This tactical interdiction effort and the air support activities associated with it produced immediate results during the first half of 1974. Seizures of marihuana, narcotics, and dangerous drugs were made with increasing frequency between ports of entry along the southern border, and the trend has continued. Since November 1, 1973, when tactical interdiction units were first established, through March 12, 1974, these units were responsible for 243 arrests and the seizure of 87,827 pounds of marihuana, 2,473 pounds of hashish, 4.8 pounds of heroin, 51 pounds of cocaine, 128 vehicles, 10 vessels; 1 aircraft; over $94,000 worth of currency; and $106,000 of general merchandise. Mere statistics? Not at all. These figures represent a significant setback for the smuggler, and a real threat to his existence. "We will continue," said Commissioner Acree, "to develop new techniques and improvements in our tactical interdiction effort, with the objective of

The modernization of Customs has also meant the use of helicopters and light aircraft to keep pace with the technology employed by smugglers. Aircraft increase the range and speed of Customs search and surveillance activities and are particularly well suited to operations in coastal areas and over large areas of sparsely settled country.

Mobile land radar units like this one are very effective day or night over flat terrain and have immensely increased the effectiveness of border patrol officers.

Customs officers aboard one of the service's fast patrol boats in the Falcom Dam area of Texas near the Mexican border. This region has been a problem area for Customs, and modern high-speed boats have helped in curtailing drug smuggling and the entry of illegal aliens.

A STOL (Short Take Off and Landing) aircraft makes a steep climb-out from a small field near Nogales along the Arizona-Mexican border. The development of aircraft like this one, which can operate out of very small clearings almost anywhere in the desert, has further complicated the job of Customs in recent years and vastly increased the territory it must patrol.

Customs officers setting up special sensing devices, capable of detecting and identifying moving objects, at strategic locations along the Texas-Mexican border.

raising the cost to the smuggler of doing business to the point where it hopefully will just no longer be profitable.''

This increased activity along the borders forced smugglers to resort to the mathematical odds and attempt to smuggle their contraband through normal inspection points at ports of entry. The immediate result was an increase in the numbers and size of seizures at these locations.

Customs analyzed the 1973 seizure statistics and developed a special enforcement program to cope with the Mexican marihuana harvest. Results of "Operation Harvest" were little short of spectacular. In the first three weeks, Customs seized over 15 tons of marihuana, 53 vehicles, and arrested 45 persons.

Thousands of square miles of remote countryside near the U.S.–Mexican border are all but impossible for Customs to patrol adequately, but special vehicles and mobile units have made the task more manageable and have made remote border crossing a risky proposition for smugglers.

New Ports and Stations

New highways and bridges into Canada and Mexico, new technology involving long-range, wide-bodied aircraft and modern containerized-cargo ships, changes in trade and commerce, continue to make new Customs ports and stations a highly valued economic asset to communities. The commissioner receives requests in an endless stream from governors, congressmen, and Chambers of Commerce to establish new Customs ports or stations in response to the dynamics of world trade. However, because of limited resources he has been able to honor comparatively few of these requests. On July 1, 1973, he opened a new port at Charleston, West Virginia. A new port was opened at Fresno, California, in January 1974, and another at Wichita, Kansas, in April. He was able to provide twenty-four-hour Customs service at Raymond, Montana, effective January 21, 1974, thus expediting the movement of fuel, diesel oil, and gasoline from Canada

An increase in small commuter airlines and private aircraft crossing the border and operating from small airfields without facilities has forced Customs to improvise at these remote ports of entry. This is a one bench Customs inspection station on a dirt strip near Presidio, Texas.

The loading and unloading of ship cargo has
been revolutionized in recent years with
the introduction of modular cargo containers
that can be placed directly on special flatbed
trucks. These containers are about forty
feet long, and when loaded each one may
hold up to twenty-five tons of material.
The containers are sealed until Customs
inspection. A vessel loaded in this way can
be completely unloaded in ten hours.

into eastern Montana and western North Dakota. The Canadian Customs Service has provided twenty-four-hour service at Regway, Saskatchewan, which is the Canadian port across from Raymond.

To illustrate the spiraling work load confronting the U.S. Customs Service today, a summary of its operations during fiscal 1974 reveals that the Service seized more than $423 million worth of illegal drugs and narcotics, including record quantities of cocaine, polydrugs (amphetamines, barbiturates, and so on), and marihuana. The figure was about twice the agency's total operating budget for the year, and is not included in the revenue it collected, approximately $4.25 billion. More than $80.2 billion worth of imported merchandise was processed through Customs in the same year, up 30 percent over 1973.

The number of tourists, travelers, and others clearing through Customs climbed 9 percent, from 247 million in 1973 to a record total of 267 million in 1974, far greater than the total population of the United States. This figure includes Americans traveling abroad; foreign tourists visiting the U.S.A.; the movement of military and government personnel; laborers crossing back and forth across the Mexican border on a regular basis, and so on. More than 75 million land vehicles, including cars, trucks, buses, plus an additional 120,000 ships and 347,000 aircraft, also cleared through Customs.

The Treasury Enforcement Communications System (TECS), the Customs Service's nationwide computer-based lookout and communications system, accounted for 1,700 arrests and detentions, more than double the 839 "hits" of the previous year.

Commercial fraud cases investigated by Customs during the year rose sharply, with 4,905 cases closed in 1974, an increase of 33 percent. Another 4,250 active cases were carried over into the new fiscal year 1975, which began on July 1, 1974.

How Customs Technology
Guards the Nation's Business

The Customs Law Enforcement Data Processing Division serves the agency with a variety of computer programs for compiling, maintaining, and retrieving intelligence. The first and best-known system is CADPIN (Customs Automatic Data Processing Intelligence Network), later changed to TECS (Treasury Enforcement Communications System), by which records of known and suspected smugglers and their vehicles are quickly distributed to terminals located across the country. Additional intelligence files are maintained on computer tape, and programs are being developed for increasingly sophisticated methods of data processing.

The TECS Computer Center, which services all Treasury agencies, is located in San Diego, California, and contains the most modern data processing equipment in the world, protected by elaborate security and fire-control systems. There are two computers, advanced Burroughs B5500 dual processors. Each of these machines is like two computers in one. If Processor A is overworking, it will automatically call in Processor B to take over some of the load. TECS operates twenty-four hours a day and is never "off the air."

Data communication processors (DCPs) police the messages going into the 5500s. They check incoming signals and voltage levels. When the message is

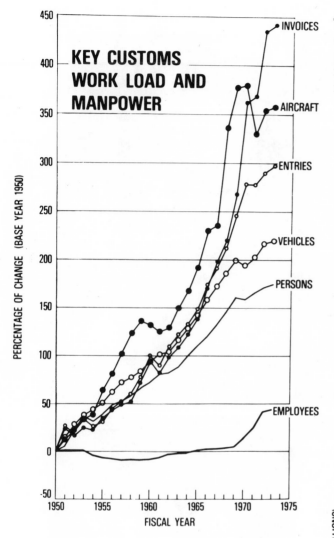

This graph vividly shows the remarkable efficiency of the Customs service, with its skyrocketing work load over the last twenty-five years compared to its relatively small increase in manpower.

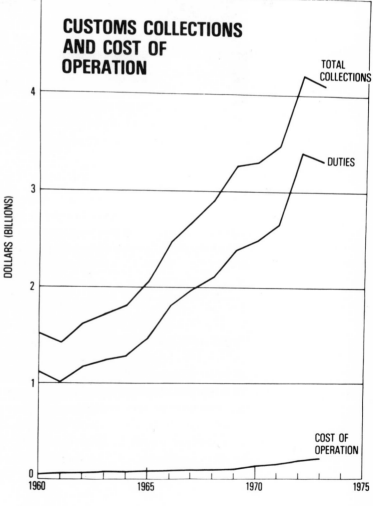

The Customs service has always enjoyed the reputation of an excellent revenue producer for the government, bringing in far more than it spends in its operations. As this graph shows, this is still true today.

The Treasury Enforcement Communications System (TECS) is the new system of nation-wide computers and interrogators that provides local Customs inspectors with important information about individuals and vehicles entering the United States. The computers are linked to the information systems of the FBI, many state, county, and local police departments, and Interpol. The interrogating equipment is relatively small and easy to operate, and it can be installed at ports of entry and land border crossings, or even in special vehicles that are used for surveillance in remote areas.

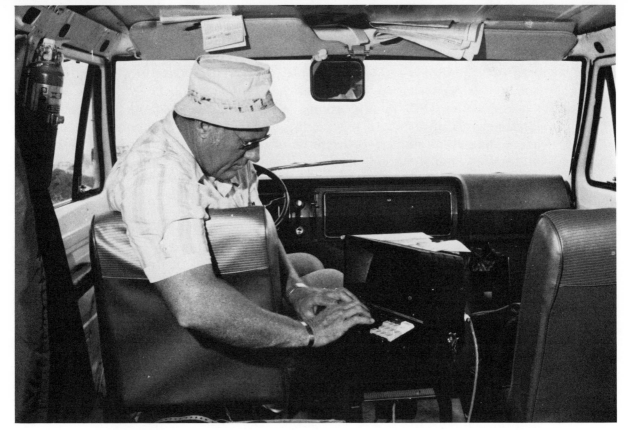

complete, they pass it on to the computers. They also inhibit a computer from sending messages to a terminal while that terminal is communicating with the computer. One DCP can service up to 255 terminals connected to the 5500.

The 1975 budget for TECS was $7 million, but it paid off in seizures and arrests whose monetary value would be many times that. With a staff of more than eighty now, the Law Enforcement Systems Division directs the TECS system. It includes branches which oversee the hardware—the computer equipment itself—and the program, the "software," which tells the hardware what information to process and how.

TECS went into operation in April 1970, with twenty-three terminals in California. There are now some six hundred terminals located at ports of entry along both borders and at special Offices of Enforcement around the country. Queries of TECS records can be made at two types of terminals—primary and secondary. Primary terminals are located only at traffic lanes at border ports of entry. Only license plate numbers can be queried here. As each vehicle enters this country, an inspector types the license number on the terminal keyboard and, in a fraction of a second, the terminal responds negatively, or it repeats the license number, giving its year and state if known, and types out such vital information about the owner as "armed and dangerous." Simultaneously, a terminal at the secondary inspection area prints out the entire record of the vehicle, including its make, year, color, and persons associated with it. This complete record is available by the time the vehicle arrives there for further inspection.

Secondary terminals have other capabilities. In addition to license plate numbers, they can be queried on names and aliases. Response time on these queries averages six to ten seconds.

In 1973, queries at primary terminals averaged 318,000 a week. On July 4 some 304,000 primary queries were made in a twenty-four-hour period. In 1972, 686 productive TECS identifications were received in the field. They resulted in total seizures of about 13,483 pounds of marihuana, 287 pounds of hashish, 31 pounds of heroin, 1,566,481 units of dangerous drugs and other drugs and undeclared items. As the result of these identifications, 444 suspects were arrested or detained by Customs and turned over to other agencies.

A recent TECS identification points up the remarkable value of the system as an enforcement tool. In the course of surveillance of a Los Angeles–area drug smuggling group, about 15 vehicles suspected of being "load cars" were identified. TECS records on each of the vehicles were entered by the Sector Intelligence Unit in Los Angeles. One of these vehicles, a 1951 Cadillac, entered the country at San Ysidro and, after an inspector verified the license number and referred the vehicle for secondary inspection, about 322,000 Seconal capsules (a barbiturate) were found in secret compartments in the door panels. The 30 bags of "red devils" weighed some 77 pounds.

A system similar to TECS was put into operation in July 1973 for the Office of Drug Abuse Law Enforcement (DALE), an agency formed early in 1972 to utilize the resources of federal, state, and local agencies in combating drug traffic. The DALE system contained records of known and suspected smugglers. Eventually it was absorbed by the Drug Enforcement Administration.

New computer programs, which will also be used to benefit TECS, are constantly being tested. The number of available scan lines has been greatly increased, allowing for more extensive record keeping. Computer systems for the Internal Revenue Service and other agencies of Treasury are also being developed. There are monthly printouts of total arrests and seizures reported by each of the agency offices. These include breakdowns by nationality, age of the subject, the port of entry, conveyance, method of concealment, and a description of and amount of the seizure. Each printout is sent to the office concerned and enables that office to quickly spot smuggling trends.

The TECS system is hooked up with the Federal Bureau of Investigation's National Crime Information Center (NCIC), which contains about four million records of vehicles and license plates, boats, wanted persons, stolen articles and securities, and guns, in addition to criminal histories. It is now possible to query records in any of these categories at secondary TECS terminals.

The number of TECS stations along the Canadian border and at International airports is being increased and the first terminal has been installed in San Juan, Puerto Rico.

A new type of primary terminal program is in effect at Miami International Airport. The names of all travelers from abroad are queried as they approach Customs inspection, with suspicious identifications listed at the inspection area for reference.

To make TECS data more accessible to agents working in the field, teletype keyboards have been installed in their automobiles and aircraft. Because each data communication processor can handle a maximum of 255 terminals linked to its computer, minicomputers are being installed at field locations and at the computer center. The minicomputer processes queries from primary terminals in its area, and has just one line leading to a computer in San Diego.

Information in TECS files is rigidly controlled, but may be released to other law-enforcement agencies with a legitimate need for it by the Assistant Commissioner for Investigations, his Deputy, the Director of the Intelligence Division, the chiefs of the Sector Intelligence Units, or special agents in charge. Other special agents may do so only in emergency situations. Requests from other than law-enforcement organizations for TECS data and requests for information from other computer files have to be made to the Director of Intelligence in Washington.

Applying the Third-Agency Rule, information released by Customs to another organization cannot be released to a third agency without the prior knowledge and consent of the Office of Investigations, and information in Customs files that was provided by another organization will not be released by Customs without the prior knowledge and consent of the source agency. The rights and privileges of privacy are rigidly respected and safeguards strictly enforced. TECS is a major tool for the protection of the American people.

The World's Second Worst Smuggling Problem: Looted Art Objects

Operating quietly, without fanfare or publicity, the Customs Office of Investigations has been carrying out a global campaign aimed at putting a stop to the smuggling of plundered artifacts and stolen art objects into the United States, where they fetch astronomical prices from collectors and galleries. Besides their intrinsic value, they have become a hedge against the galloping inflation enveloping most countries, acknowledged to be infinitely "safer" than stocks as an investment, with a potential for unlimited growth in their resale value.

John A. Grieco, Customs Senior Special Agent in charge of New York's Art Recovery Investigative Program, says: "To our knowledge, next to the traffic in narcotics, the traffic in stolen art is the biggest international crime in volume."

Customs has waged a protracted and bitter struggle against these twentieth-century pirates, who pillage ancient sites and museums for priceless paintings, Cambodian stone deities, African carved idols, Indian bronzes, pre-Columbian stelae, and so on, but the agency's powers had been severely limited by lack of power to prosecute. The Art Recovery Investigative Program was extended from New York to nationwide scope, on the heels of the international furor over the enormous rise in the international traffic in looted objects, coupled with the escalation in prices and the value placed on them.

Not until March 1971 did the United States–Mexico treaty on the importation of art objects and artifacts, providing for the recovery and return of stolen archeological, historical, and cultural properties, go into effect. The U.S. government enacted legislation as recently as June 1973 to provide for the seizure and return of any pre-Columbian monuments, murals, and sculptures exported from Mexico without the express and written permission of the Mexican government.

The laws governing the exportation of cultural treasures differ from country to country. Mexican laws are tough and the Mexicans are determined to preserve their greatest cultural resources. Some nations, such as Tunisia, have never enacted legislation to hold onto their national historic treasures. Many have discouraged the sale or export of artifacts or forbidden it, but their enforcement is feeble or nonexistent.

The U.S. Customs Art Recovery Investigative Unit has assigned a number of handpicked agents to register for art courses at New York University and other schools for intensive study of the subject. Hard-nosed investigators who complete these courses satisfactorily are then assigned to special squads which follow up on leads and tips provided by Interpol (the International Criminal Police Organization) and UNESCO (the United Nations Educational, Scientific and Cultural Organization), which have recently developed a renewed interest in stolen objects of art. Their most spectacular case to date involved a pre-Columbian piece so rare that there are only three others like it in the entire world: a Mayan bark picture book discovered only three years ago. It was retrieved from a dealer in New York and returned to Mexico by U.S. Customs.

In 1974, a Utrillo painting valued at $14,000 that had been smuggled into the U.S. was identified by Interpol as having been stolen from a European dealer. When the shop owner in New York who had purchased it was contacted by Customs, he readily returned it to Customs, who arranged for its return.

The record books abound with stories of recovery and return, frequently with the full cooperation of American dealers who unwittingly purchased the art

This Koran, dating from the ninth or tenth
century, and valued at $12,000, was one of
ten Moslem holy books stolen from a shrine
in Iran in 1969. Alerted by the International
Criminal Police Organization (Interpol),
Customs eventually tracked the book down,
and two years later it was returned to Iran.

object, unaware of its origin or the legality of how it was acquired. There was the
case of the stone jaguar from the Olmec culture, which flourished in Mexico
between 800 and 200 B.C. The cooperation of U.S. Customs was requested by its
Mexican counterpart. Importers were checked; the jaguar was found and the New
York dealer sacrificed his purchase price to return it. On January 30, 1974, the
stone jaguar was shipped in a United States plane to Mexico City, where the U.S.
ambassador, in a short ceremony, turned it over to the Mexican Cultural Minister.

Later that year, Mexican police, acting on information provided by U.S.
Customs, arrested a resident of Baltimore and charged him with the illegal
possession, transportation, and export of archeological monuments. It was
alleged that this one individual had illegally acquired more than 450 objects of
art.

The U.S. attorney general was empowered by the 1971 treaty to prosecute
those who do not legally import art objects, but it is the Customs Service upon

which our government depends to recover these objects. Complicating the problem is the question of determining whether an art work has been exported illegally from the country of origin. Certain governments work in close cooperation with the U.S.A. in the current crackdown on the pillaging of national cultural treasures; they have joined in the 1971 United States–Mexican Treaty, and their export prohibitions are made known to U.S. Customs. These countries now include Bolivia, British Honduras, Colombia, Costa Rica, the Dominican Republic, El Salvador, Guatemala, Honduras, Mexico, Panama, Peru, and Venezuela.

Another complication is the inability of Customs agents to apply the 1973 statute to objects shipped here previously; however, if there is a suspicion that an import was undervalued, or not declared, or the "country of origin" misrepresented, an investigation can be launched into any imported object. An example is the bronze sculpture of an Indian deity, imported into the U.S. by a West Coast millionaire who paid $1 million to a dealer for its possession. Known as the *Nataraja*, the piece was requested by the government of India. U.S. Customs initiated an investigation into the circumstances of its importation. At this time of writing, the case had not been closed. But if a finding should be made of *misdeclaration* (to Customs), a penalty could be imposed equal to the value of the *Nataraja*, one million dollars.

Antiques that are one hundred years old and ethnographic objects more than fifty years old are free of customs duty, but they must be declared upon arrival in

An appraiser's aide here tries to determine whether or not this suit of armor qualifies as a genuine antique.

How would Customs officials determine the value of this object, a huge granite block, part of the first shipment of stones that made up the old London Bridge, brought to this country in 1968?

the United States. An antique which is only 99 years old is dutiable. A "work of art" can be a painting or sculpture which represents an original concept, done entirely by hand—the key word is "original."

New York City is the center for international traffic in art objects and other cultural artifacts. Highly trained, nationally known specialists determine whether cultural importations meet the test of antiquity. They do their work at ports of entry, piers, airports, warehouses, antique shops, and at the appraiser's stores, formerly located for many years at 201 Varick Street, Manhattan, and later moved to the World Trade Center. These specialists share spacious facilities with a host of other import specialists in Customs Region II (New York), who are experts in a fantastically wide range of subjects such as diamonds, rugs, textiles, musical instruments, agricultural products, and eighty-five others including bull semen. "Wanted lists," which are published by various countries, are used to guide the Customs import specialists and appraisers.

Art objects are commonly used to conceal narcotics, and import specialists are alert to this possibility. Not long ago, a verifier, who checks to see that invoices correspond with shipments and their contents, was looking over bongo drums in a package from West Africa. He tapped the drums. They failed to bong properly. He opened them, only to find they were stuffed with marihuana.

Customs Detector Dogs

The introduction in 1970 of highly trained detector dogs as a major tool in the interdiction of drug smuggling was a fresh, innovative step in the work of the U.S. Customs Service. Dogs have proved their effectiveness in identifying marihuana and hashish, its concentrated derivative, particularly in mail parcels and cargo shipped into the United States from abroad, and also in vehicles arriv-

Customs now has at its disposal specially
trained dogs capable of sniffing out
marihuana, hashish, and in some cases even
heroin. These animals are used to examine
mail parcels, vehicles, and so on, but they
are not used to search human beings.

ing at border stations such as San Ysidro, Calexico, Laredo, El Paso, and other points.

The basic policy governing the use of these dogs was to keep them *away from people*, concentrating exclusively on mail parcels and cargo, in ships, vehicles, aircraft both private and commercial, buses, and trucks, but *never* on persons no matter who they were. This policy has remained and will doubtless remain unchanged, in order to protect innocent people and even smugglers from personal injury.

German shepherds and Labrador retrievers were purchased by Customs from the military and from private individuals. They were originally trained by former U.S. Army dog handlers who were recruited by the U.S. Customs Service under special arrangement with the Department of Defense. In fact, early discharge from the army was offered as an inducement to GIs who were interested in joining the program as Civil Service employees. The excellent facilities at Lackland Air Force Base in Texas were used by Customs to train the first twelve dogs and six handlers, inaugurating the program during Commissioner Johnson's term in office. Johnson's successor, Myles J. Ambrose, was so enthusiastic over the program that he issued a statement expressing the belief that: "With expanded use of trained dogs, I believe we can halt the entry of marihuana through the Mexican border."

The program was under the overall supervision of a veteran Air Force instructor and military police sergeant named Gene McEathron, who had made a reputation as the author of "personality tests" for the canines. These profiles enabled dog trainers to identify certain traits required in conditioning the animals for the work they had to do. The only dogs selected for Customs training were those who were judged to have a "gentle disposition." However, later events proved that some of these "gentle" animals brought grief to their trainers. One trainer lost his earlobe, and another a finger, to overenthusiastic dogs. But such incidents were rare.

Training for each dog and handler takes approximately two months. Initially, Customs officers instruct the handler in Customs laws, procedures, and search techniques. Then a training program matching each dog handler with two dogs is set up. During this phase, the dogs learn to identify concealed marihuana and the handler learns to respond to each dog's method of alerting him.

Prior to "graduation," the dogs must successfully complete intensive tests. One involves the finding of marihuana concealed among parcels of foodstuffs, heavily disguised by odor-masking chemicals. In one of the tests, marihuana is buried in a fruit jar under a gravel road. The dog must walk along the road, locate the jar, and dig it up.

Once training is completed, narcotic detector dog teams are assigned to Customs international mail facilities, cargo docks and terminals, and border ports, where they screen mail, cargo, unaccompanied baggage, ships, and vehicles suspected of carrying illicit drugs. Dogs are being successfully employed at many ports of entry throughout the country.

During one two-week trial period, the dogs made eighteen seizures of illicit drugs. Huge numbers of packages were opened during the trial period. In no case was any marihuana found in the packages that the dogs had passed. In no case did the dogs fail to detect control packages of drugs planted among the mail parcels. Today detector dogs are responsible for thousands of seizures. It takes a dog sixty seconds to detect and indicate the presence of marihuana in a vehicle. The same search by a trained professional inspector requires at least twenty minutes.

On his first test assignment in Laredo, Texas, a Customs detector dog indicated that marihuana was concealed behind the door panel of a previously searched car. The marihuana was so skillfully disguised that the Customs officers found no indication that the door panel had been tampered with. When the panel was removed, five pounds of marihuana were found and two smugglers were arrested.

In Miami, when a Customs dog pawed the surface of a wooden table he indicated the presence of hashish. Officers polished out the scratch marks and sent the table, under surveillance, to the addressee. When the table was disassembled, twenty pounds of hashish were seized and the violator arrested.

So impressive were the performances of the Customs detector dogs, that an invitation came from the White House to have one of these outstanding canines show his stuff in the presence of the President. Arrangements were made for a demonstration on the back lawn of the White House with the Chief Executive, his top staff, and the White House Press Corps in attendance. Kishi was elected for the assignment.

In the fall of 1971 Kishi was flown in from his duty station on the California–Mexican border along with Albert from Texas, and their Customs handler. A huge pile of unscreened and unopened foreign mail parcels were spread out on the lawn. As the President looked on, with television cameras and reporters riveting their attention on this unusual event, Kishi and Albert went sniffing through the mail parcels. In a few minutes, Kishi called attention to a package that, when opened, revealed a three-inch-thick candle into which several ounces of contraband hashish had been stuffed.

Needless to say, Kishi and Albert made front page headlines all over the country, and the entire performance was shown on television screens in millions of homes throughout the U.S.

During 1967, their first year on the job, detector dogs sniffed out more than three million dollars in narcotics and other illegal drugs. The Service by now had forty-two dogs and twenty-eight handlers working at twenty-two ports of entry. During this period approximately 1,800,000 mail packages were examined, 4,000 vehicles screened, and 100,000 cargo units inspected.

A major breakthrough occurred when, a few months later, the country was told that certain carefully selected and highly trained dogs had been taught to identify two of the most potent narcotics, heroin and cocaine, which had hitherto been beyond the powers of the canine olfactory nerves. Marihuana and hashish, which emit overpowering odors, were readily identifiable, but heroin and "coke," the scourge of the country's drug epidemic, had up until now defied detection.

One of the most dramatic episodes in the story of Customs detector dogs took place in a Philadelphia courtroom where a black Labrador retriever named Wanda presented evidence that helped convict two drug smugglers.

Wanda, formerly assigned to the District Director's office in Philadelphia and handled by Customs dog handler Dave McKinney, was responsible for the seizure of approximately forty-five pounds of hashish and one pound of opium at the Philadelphia International Airport in September 1973.

When two men fitting the hijacker profile attempted to board an aircraft bound for San Francisco, Customs security officers found a small piece of hashish in one of the men's pockets.

One suspect was arrested by the officers, had his bags removed from the aircraft, while the other man was allowed to board. Customs special agents were notified of the arrest and proceeded to the airport.

After an investigation, the special agents called for McKinney and Wanda. When Wanda examined the two bags of the man who was detained, her reaction was instantaneous. Based on facts discovered during the investigation and Wanda's reaction, a search warrant was obtained and the contraband seized. Another warrant was issued for the second suspect who was arrested in San Francisco as he walked off the aircraft.

Defense lawyers for the two men would not stipulate to Wanda's ability to detect hashish; Wanda and McKinney were subpoenaed to a hearing. The defense requested that Wanda identify hashish concealed among a number of empty boxes. The animal detected the hashish three times for the Court. Inspector McKinney testified that Wanda had made about forty identifications of narcotics while assigned to the Philadelphia office. He said that she had provided "probable cause" for at least two search warrants. It was the first time a detector dog had been used in a court case.

While the detector dog plan is a comparatively recent development in the war on narcotics, the Treasury Department had a genuine "watchdog of the Treasury" many years ago. Early in the nineteenth century, Henry Voight, Chief Coiner of the first United States Mint at Philadelphia, sponsored a dog called Nero. The Bureau of the Mint paid $3 for the animal.

Old handwritten Treasury ledgers record expenditures for Nero and his successors, including payments for food and license tags. The owners or handlers also received allowances for their work, including a rum allowance ranging from $1 to $3 per month. There was a considerable fuss in 1825 when new Treasury regulations trimmed the budget by ending the beverage allowance.

Special rules were laid down for Nero. Only the Bureau of the Mint watchmen were permitted to feed him. Fraternizing with the staff was prohibited. Nero accompanied the night watchman on his rounds throughout the Mint. Reports show that the dog made the rounds even when the night guard was absent.

An old Treasury seal shows a symbolic strongbox supporting a balance scale, and lying beside the sturdy vault there is a determined dog, with his left front paw securely guarding a large key. Who originated the seal is not known and how extensively it was used on early documents is also unknown. But the original plate is preserved in the Government Printing Office.

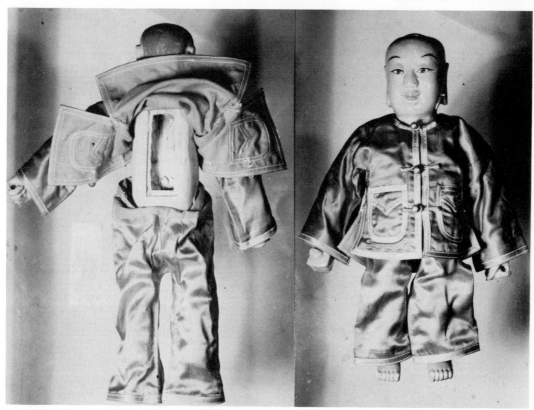

This doll was one of thirty discovered in
Hong Kong in 1954. The small hollowed-out
cavity was designed to conceal jewels or
small gold bars.

A classic smuggler's device, the hollowed-
out book.

chapter six

War without
Beginning or End

Most history books either ignore the U.S. Customs Service altogether or gloss over its unique contribution to American history under the prosaic heading of the Tariff laws of the United States. And yet this arm of the Treasury Department, reaching out across the continent from ocean to ocean and border to border, has a story of its own that is every bit as dramatic as the richly chronicled history of the army, the navy, the air force, or the FBI.

One facet of this story is the eternal war on the smuggling of contraband—narcotics, gold, watch movements, embargoed merchandise from hostile countries, and a long list of other prohibited or regulated articles.

Unlike other conflicts in which the forces of this country have participated, the war on smuggling is a war without beginning or end. It was waged by the British to enforce their own list of contraband articles. During the colonial period, smuggling was regarded as an act of patriotism in defiance of His Britannic Majesty's authority. It is being conducted today by infinitely more ingenious and resourceful smugglers, intent upon defrauding the Treasury and reaping huge profits at the expense of the people.

The American people have received, through books and other publications, mass circulation newspapers and magazines, and radio and television, only the tip of the iceberg. The full story of the offensive against smugglers, both professional and amateur, is one which probably can never be completely told. It is an ongoing contest between the forces of government and the smugglers, each side forever striving to outwit and outmaneuver the other. The human imagination has no boundaries, and there are virtually no ends to which the professional smuggler will not go in seeking to get his cargo to its destination.

The variety of contraband is as great as are the methods of bringing it into the country, proving once again that greed has no nationality, nor is it confined to the people of any race, creed, color, or sex, or even to their material resources. The rich as well as the poor have been apprehended trying to get by Customs barriers with undervalued merchandise. Men as well as women are intercepted, fined, arrested, and sentenced to long prison terms on smuggling charges. Not even the rich and famous are above trying to cheat the Customs.

The vehicles and devices employed in smuggling range from automobiles, boats, aircraft, and even natural body cavities, to tape recorders, women's girdles, wigs, trouser cuffs, and so on—there is virtually no limit to the ingenuity employed to cheat the government of its revenues. It has been said that there are 4,000 potential places of concealment in one modern passenger ship alone.

Another very common smuggler's tool, the suitcase with the false bottom.

A Customs inspector at the National Training Center at Hofstra University demonstrates how small objects can be concealed in the heel of a shoe.

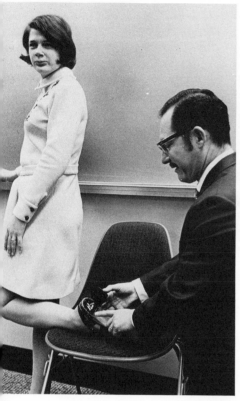

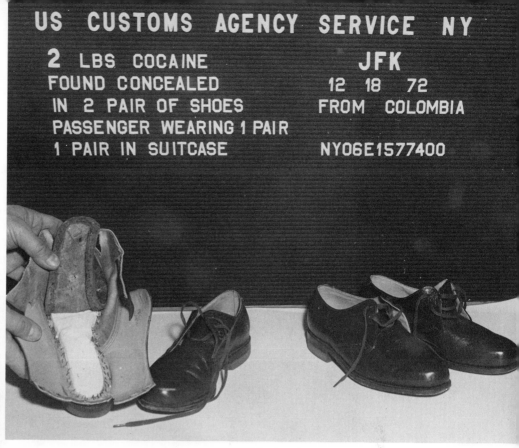

US CUSTOMS AGENCY SERVICE NY
2 LBS COCAINE   JFK
FOUND CONCEALED   12 18 72
IN 2 PAIR OF SHOES   FROM COLOMBIA
PASSENGER WEARING 1 PAIR
1 PAIR IN SUITCASE   NYO6E1577400

Customs agents at John F. Kennedy International Airport discovered about two pounds of cocaine hidden in the soles of two pairs of shoes belonging to a passenger arriving from Colombia. One pair was worn by the passenger, and the other was found in his suitcase.

About 750 grams of cocaine were discovered by Miami Customs inspectors in the frames of two religious pictures.

Customs agents were informed and waiting
when the wearer of this artificial leg arrived
in New York from Latin America. It was
full of marihuana.

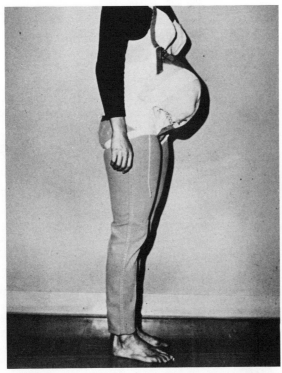

This false pregnancy cage is a very common
means of smuggling narcotics into the
country.

Illegally imported fireworks revealed
themselves to Customs inspectors rather
dramatically when they exploded inside the
truck that was carrying them.

Perhaps the most popular device used for smuggling is the motor vehicle,
especially along border crossings, but also popular is the concealment of contraband in cars being transported by ship from foreign countries. Virtually every
section of the car is utilized by smugglers in their relentless attempts to evade
Customs. For example, inspectors confiscated 7.5 million mini-amphetamine
tablets concealed in a specially built secret compartment of a car's trunk; the pills
were wrapped in plastic bags. Another 4.5 million pills had been solidly packed
in false compartments in the automobile's front fenders. In another case, illicit
pills were discovered in the car's spare tire, and in yet another case behind the
firewall of a vehicle. Smugglers also use the door panels, the areas behind rear
seats, the dashboard, the engine compartment, false ceilings in campers, tubeless
tires, the engine's air cleaner, and so on.

Some of the situations confronted by Customs inspectors are intriguing. There
was the case of the driver of a pickup truck arriving from Mexico, who laconically
told Customs inspectors: "I brought you guys a couple of bags of marihuana.
They're in the back." He told the officers that he had fourteen children of his own,
that seven of them were in school, and that he wanted to help U.S. Customs keep
marihuana out of the country and away from all children. He was released with
thanks, and Customs kept the marihuana.

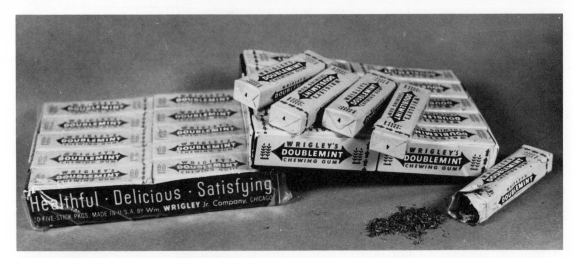

These "healthful, delicious, satisfying" packages of chewing gum were filled with marihuana. They were discovered in Philadelphia and traced back to Vietnam.

The hardcover bindings of these encyclopedia volumes, brought into the country by two women on a flight from Colombia, contained five pounds of cocaine.

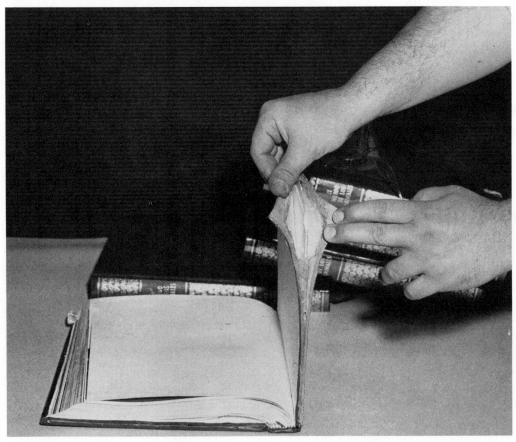

The larger vessel in this photograph, the converted World War II freighter *Don Miguel,* had been featured in the motion picture *Mr. Roberts.* But here it is being towed into Los Angeles by the *San Jorge* after developing engine trouble. Both vessels, registered to the same owner in Mexico, were seized, and aboard the *Don Miguel* Customs agents discovered seven tons of marihuana concealed under crates of ground coffee.

The lining of this woman's coat was packed with marihuana.

The finger cavities of this bowling ball were used to conceal one-half a kilo, or a little over a pound, of cocaine.

A New Mexico state policeman observed a camper driving on the wrong side of the road and stopped it. The responses to his questions aroused his suspicions, and he requested permission to search the vehicle. When the permission was denied, he radioed for another officer. One of the occupants of the camper was placed in a vehicle with one of the policemen, and the other was instructed to drive the camper to a place of inspection, where it was discovered to be a huge rolling tobacco can with refined marihuana and cigarette papers in it. A search warrant was obtained, and thirty large plastic bags of marihuana were located, with a gross weight of 1,250 pounds. The men were turned over to a Customs agent and held under bonds of $200,000 each. The truck and marihuana were seized.

False gas tanks like this one are often filled with drugs and installed on cars driven into the country from Mexico. The tank is designed to hold just enough actual gas to drive from the point of departure to some point just across the border.

Inside the upholstery of the seat of this automobile, Customs inspectors discovered a large quantity of illegally imported watch movements.

This motorcycle seat, shipped from Spain, just didn't feel right to a Detroit Customs inspector. Inside were eight pounds of hashish.

The marihuana pictured here has been pressed into thin sheets, made rigid with an unknown cohesive, and then placed in plastic envelopes inside these long-playing record jackets. This material was seized by Customs agents in Chicago in 1971.

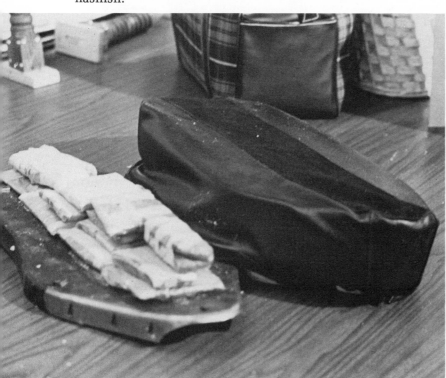

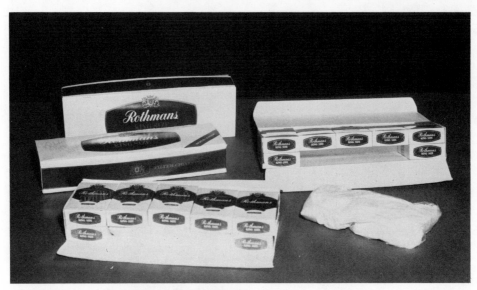

These four cartons of English cigarettes,
seized at John F. Kennedy International
Airport in 1972, were found to contain two
kilos of cocaine, concealed in packets under
the top layer of cigarettes.

This Jamaican wood carving, brought into
Louisiana in 1972, aroused the suspicions of
one of Customs' specially trained dogs.
When cut open, it was found to have been
stuffed with about five pounds of marihuana.

A shipment of straw-covered, false-bottomed
wine jugs, like the one shown here, was
brought into the country from Argentina.
Seized in New York, they were found to
contain a quantity of heroin valued at close
to two million dollars at street prices.

This is one of two swimsuits, worn as
undergarments by two women arriving in
Miami from Colombia, each of which was
found to contain about eight pounds of
marihuana sewn into the lining.

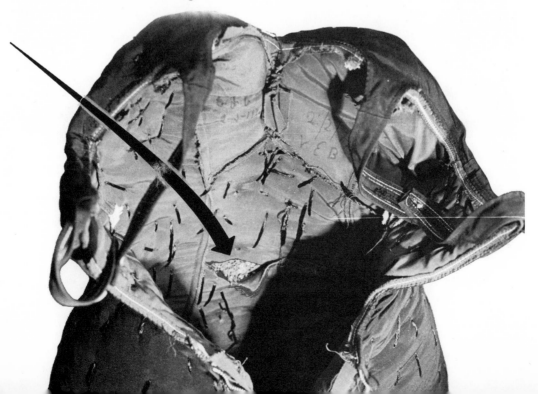

This Mondrian-style paper collage painting, sent from Amsterdam and destined for New Orleans, didn't fool Customs inspectors working in a New York mail room. The papier mâché elements contained almost one and a half pounds of hashish.

This bronze bust, seized at Philadelphia, contained ninety-two pounds of hashish. Like many other objects seized by Customs, it was subsequently repacked, released, and watched, so that the receivers of narcotics in this country can be traced and arrested. The "shadowing" of this bust, as well as a narcotics-laden Venus de Milo that arrived at Philadelphia a day later, eventually led to the uncovering of a small but ambitious smuggling ring and the arrest of four individuals here and in Europe.

These dishes, shipped from Nepal, to San Francisco, are nothing more than bricks of compressed hashish.

This bronze Buddha was found in a false-bottomed trunk seized in Los Angeles. It was part of a large shipment of oriental art objects that had been hollowed out and stuffed with close to a quarter of a million dollars' worth of lumps of hashish.

An arrival from Jamaica at Miami Airport was carrying a five-gallon can of berry juice. Customs officials opened the can and discovered that it really contained fifteen pounds of marihuana.

A Customs inspector at Port Huron, Michigan, was credited with the largest single seizure of hashish in the Michigan area, when he picked up twenty pounds from a passenger traveling by train from Montreal, Canada, to Port Huron. The hashish was hidden in a briefcase under an overcoat on the baggage rack above the passenger's seat, and also taped to his legs and hidden by his boots. The smuggler was returning from a trip to Europe and the Middle East and had flown from Brussels to Montreal.

When Customs officials in the mail division in California found a total of ninety-two pounds of marihuana concealed in two packages mailed from Korea, they arranged for a "controlled delivery." With the assistance of the U.S. Army, the Post Office, and Los Angeles Police Narcotics officers, the delivery was made. Two arrests and the seizure of a car resulted.

Four stereo speakers containing approximately twenty-five pounds of hashish were sent from Frankfurt, Germany, to addresses in Connecticut. The packages were intercepted in New York, and two of them delivered under supervision. Two men were arrested.

A jewelry salesman deplaned at Tucson, Arizona, but failed to declare the items he brought with him. Customs officials located thirteen diamonds, rubies and pearls as well as two wooden statues. All were confiscated.

The search of two Los Angeles International Airport arrivals disclosed undeclared jewelry worth $13,000. Included were a pair of earrings, thirty-five rings, nine key rings, four pendants, and ten packages of opals, approximately four hundred to the package. Customs seized the jewelry and made two arrests.

This diving cylinder belonged to a passenger returning to the states from Jamaica. When the valve was removed, Customs inspectors removed eight and a half pounds of marihuana.

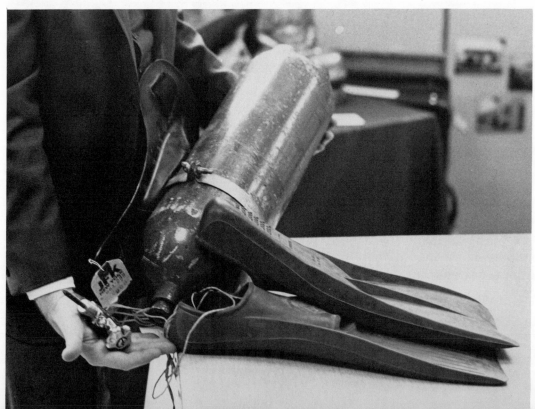

Detectives of the Honolulu Police Department examine a large shipment of marihuana concealed in speaker cabinets. This seizure was the result of the combined efforts of Customs and local police officials. The cabinets were released in order to effect a "supervised delivery" and arrest those involved in the smuggling operation.
Courtesy *The Honolulu Advertiser.*

The examination of gift packages supposedly containing jellied fruits, candies, and cheese, and apparently shipped by a reliable English firm, uncovered a plentiful supply of hashish. An investigation by Customs disclosed that the gifts had been purchased by an American in London. He waited until the packages were ready for shipment, picked them up, and said he would mail them himself. The packages were carefully opened and hashish substituted. They were then returned to the store with the story that the purchaser had changed his mind once again. The scheme failed, thanks to the alertness of Customs officers.

Concealed in the roof of this truck was a compartment that held 354 kilos of marihuana.

Expensive perfumes and unmounted semi-precious stones are items frequently concealed to avoid payment of duty. Those pictured here were discovered in a false-bottomed suitcase.

This small vase and pewter kettle contained
valuable industrial tool bits, which
Japanese agents were attempting to smuggle
out of the country just prior to the attack
on Pearl Harbor.

Customs inspectors and special agents at the Peace Bridge in Buffalo, New York, seized 598 bottles of phenylbutazone hidden in a hearse that also contained two bodies being returned from Canada. Phenylbutazone is used as a pain-killer for horses and other large animals.

Miss Lynn Pelletier, a twenty-two-year-old U.S. Customs inspector, combined womanly curiosity and a knowledge of drug smuggling techniques in her search of a camper arriving by ship at Elizabeth, New Jersey, in 1971. She discovered 96½ pounds of heroin worth up to $12 million on the street. Miss Pelletier was awarded the Special Act or Service Award of the Bureau of Customs by Commissioner of Customs Myles J. Ambrose. Similar awards were made to Inspectors Harry Dittmyre and Larry Harris, who assisted Miss Pelletier in the discovery of the hidden heroin.

When the metal detection machine at the Los Angeles Airport "beeped" as a passenger started through, he immediately ran from the area. A Pan Am passenger representative reacting quickly caught the man. Metal clasps on the man's shoes had caused the beep, and a U.S. marshal shouted, "Get his boots!" No gun was found in the boots, but they did contain a fortune in marihuana and heroin.

A Customs port investigator thought that a man arriving by plane at Miami, Florida, was walking in a peculiar manner. A search disclosed 263 grams of marihuana between his legs and 64 grams of cocaine in his shoes.

Inspectors at Anchorage, Alaska, examined an air-freight shipment from Singapore billed as weight-lifting equipment. They discovered a large steel cylinder

The problem with drug interdiction is that only a small number of smugglers have to succeed in order to flood the country with their product. This problem is graphically illustrated in these two pictures, showing the huge amount of merchandise that can be smuggled in just one automobile or camper.

Over one hundred pounds of heroin were discovered in this commercial shipment of canned fish. A group of smugglers purchased a large quantity of the canned fish, took it to Malaga, Spain, opened some of the tins, and repacked them with heroin mixed with lead sinkers to maintain an appropriate weight. Thirteen persons were arrested in this investigation.

One of the most common, and most fool-
hardy, methods of smuggling is to wrap
contraband around the body. The six
pounds of heroin in this fifty-foot-long piece
of plastic tubing were discovered by an
alert Customs agent who "accidentally"
brushed against the suspect to confirm his
suspicions. This discovery ultimately led
to the arrest of six individuals in Hong
Kong, Honolulu, and San Francisco.

that did not appear to be a normal part of such equipment. Inside the cylinder
they found thirteen pounds of highly refined marihuana in forty packages. Each
package consisted of five bundles of twenty small paper tubes containing about
one gram each. Six indictments were returned for conspiracy to smuggle the
marihuana.

A Customs inspector at Miami Airport thought that a passenger appeared to
have too many bulges around her hips. A search disclosed two and a half pounds
of marihuana in the suspect's underclothing.

What is certainly the most heinous smuggling method imaginable—the concealment of heroin in the bodies and caskets of servicemen killed in Southeast Asia—was for many months under active investigation by the Bureau of Customs, the Bureau of Narcotics and Dangerous Drugs, the FBI, and the U.S. Army Criminal Investigation Division.

One investigation in Brooklyn is typical of the manner in which Customs officers must operate. Around seven P.M. on a warm spring evening in May 1960, Customs officer John J. Molony, working inside a shed on the Brooklyn waterfront, noticed two seamen coming off a Danish vessel recently arrived from Hong Kong. He stepped out, called to them to stop, and inquired if they had anything to declare. The two men said they had nothing, but their nervous reaction aroused the officer's suspicion and he decided to make a personal search. He hit the jackpot! Beneath the clothing of each suspect he found two silk-covered packets containing a little over a pound of white powder.

Nearby Customs agents were called and a field test was made, revealing a positive reaction for possible opium or heroin. Both seamen were taken to the office for questioning. They confessed that about six weeks before they had been employed by a Chinese resident in Hong Kong to smuggle heroin into the United States for delivery to a buyer in New York's Chinatown.

The suspects had visited the apartment of the intended purchaser the evening before, identified themselves by means of a slip of paper given to them in Hong

Opium smugglers failed in an attempt to evade mail inspection of this parcel by using a religious organization's return address and claiming that the parcel contained cans of exposed film. The fifty film cans seized actually contained fifty-nine pounds of opium.

Acting on a tip from two local fishermen, Customs officers seized this barge that had been beached at the mouth of a small creek along Florida's Gulf Coast. The barge held over 18,000 pounds of marihuana in 495 large bags. It is believed that this shipment was smuggled in from Jamaica.

Kong, and received cautious instructions as to how the narcotics should be delivered. They were to return to the apartment the following evening before nine. If delivery could not be made before that hour, the purchaser would be waiting the next night. He made it plain he would be expecting only the two seamen and would not open the door to anyone else. They stayed for dinner but refused to smoke his cigarettes, which were impregnated with heroin.

After a great deal of persuasion, both men agreed to cooperate with the agents and deliver the heroin. However, due to the length of time that transpired during the investigation, an attempt to deliver the contraband shortly before midnight was unsuccessful, because no one answered the apartment door.

When the agents learned that the seized heroin represented only half of the intended delivery they prevailed upon the men to draw a map of the officers' smoking room aboard ship showing the place of concealment. Agents then boarded the vessel and found four packets under a couch, making a grand total of four pounds of heroin, worth about $1 million on the street.

Agents spent a lively twenty hours digging up facts. Telephone company records, utility records, and lease agreements were examined. They laid their strategy. Eventually it was decided to permit the heroin to be delivered to the unknown Chinese national as they maintained electronic surveillance over the movements of the two seamen. A listening post was set up in a nearby apartment.

The seamen started out with the heroin and were monitored as they delivered the packets and received their delivery fees. Instructions for delivery of the remaining kilo believed to be aboard ship were received. As the buyer removed the locks from his door to permit their exit and wished the seamen good luck, Customs agents moved in and placed the Chinese purchaser under arrest. The heroin was recovered along with $1,600 paid in fees.

This incident on the Brooklyn waterfront was to be repeated countless times in every U.S. port of entry during the decade of the sixties and well into the first half of the seventies. The scenario varied in the cast of characters, the setting, the time frame, and the degree of suspense. But the formula seldom varied from the original.

Canvas bags, like suitcases, may also have false bottoms. This one concealed four pounds of hashish.

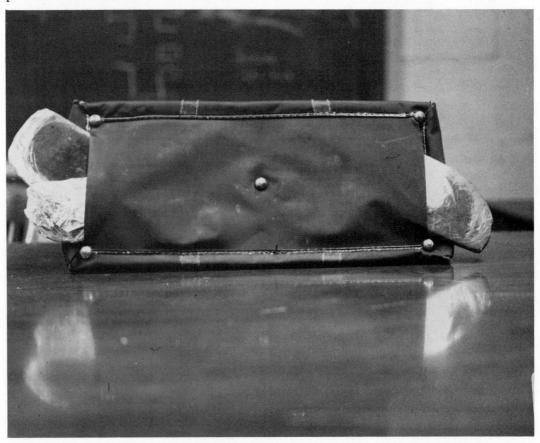

Auguste Joseph Ricord, considered at the time the major figure in the smuggling of French heroin into the United States through South America, was convicted in the Federal Southern Judicial District of New York on December 15, 1972, of conspiracy to smuggle narcotics, in one of the most dramatic cases in Customs history.

The sixty-two-year-old Argentine citizen, who was born in Marseilles, France, of Corsican parents, was sentenced to twenty years in prison and fined $20,000—the maximum penalty under federal law. In addition, he was ordered to pay the cost of his prosecution, estimated at $75,000 to $100,000. In commenting on the amount of heroin Ricord is accused of trafficking in, presiding Judge John M. Cannella said, "The end product in suffering and mortality from this quantity would probably equal the recent figures given for the war in Vietnam." It has been estimated that Ricord's organization was responsible for smuggling fifteen tons of heroin into this country over a five-year period.

Specifically, Ricord was charged with conspiracy to violate antismuggling laws, in connection with ninety-three pounds of heroin seized in October 1970. That case began when, in September of that year, the American Consul in Asuncion, Paraguay, received an anonymous letter listing light aircraft being used to smuggle heroin. The letter was forwarded to U.S. Customs. One of the planes, a Cessna 210, arrived at Miami International Airport on October 18, on a flight originating in Paraguay. It was kept under surveillance and a search of the craft disclosed ninety-three pounds of heroin in three false-bottom suitcases. The pilot and copilot were arrested.

Ricord was indicted in March 1971 and was arrested by police in Paraguay that month. He was held in jail there, fighting extradition, until September 2, 1972, when he was turned over to U.S. Customs and Justice Department agents in Asuncion, placed aboard a Pan American plane bound for New York, and arrested. He had never before been in the United States.

Testimony at the trial indicated that Ricord had given suitcases of heroin to couriers at his motel-restaurant near Asuncion and at one point received $100,000 for fifteen kilos of heroin delivered to New York in September 1970.

Old-timers recall that the seizure of a few ounces of heroin or a pound or two of marihuana made headlines in 1953. Ten years later the seizure of 172 pounds of refined marihuana, concealed in a Buick crossing over the Mexican border into the U.S. at Eagle Pass, Texas, was reported as being the largest in history. And yet in 1974 the weed was being seized by the ton. Indeed, during the year ending June 30, 1974, the Customs Service interdicted 225.4 tons of cannabis, mostly along the Mexican border, more than had been stopped during the entire decade of the sixties, and a 45 percent increase over the 1973 figure of 156 tons.

There was a marked increase in seizures of cocaine beginning in the early seventies. In the first six months of 1973, 340 pounds of it were seized by Customs, compared with ninety-eight pounds during the same period in 1972. Usually the packets were small—one or two kilos—but the number of seizures made jumped by 164 percent. In many cases, body carriers were used. However,

The ultimate fate of marihuana that is seized
by Customs. Certain quantities may be
temporarily held as evidence, but eventually
the contraband is burned.

About two tons of marihuana, the largest
amount ever seized on the East Coast, was
smuggled to Florida from Colombia aboard
the pleasure yacht *Nurmi*. The yacht was
followed back to this country by a Customs
boat and helicopter, and three men were
arrested.

in the Midwest and Far West, there was an increase of cocaine in mail parcels from South America.

The gain in cocaine seizures has been attributed both to the increasing demand and higher prices for the commodity as heroin became more scarce and cocaine use became more fashionable.

The amount of heroin seized by Customs in the first six months of 1973 (eighty-three pounds) reflected a decrease of 83 percent over the same period the year before. Actually, the number of seizures increased by six, or 2 percent. The drop in the amount of heroin seized was attributed to stronger enforcement, both in the United States and in the source and transit countries.

In spite of the legendary heroism and dedication of the Customs officers, despite the vast new technology currently in use, supplemented by intensive training in the work of detection and interdiction, smuggling flourishes today as it has done for centuries.

These bricks of hashish were found packed
between sheets of Braille reading matter
mailed from Israel.

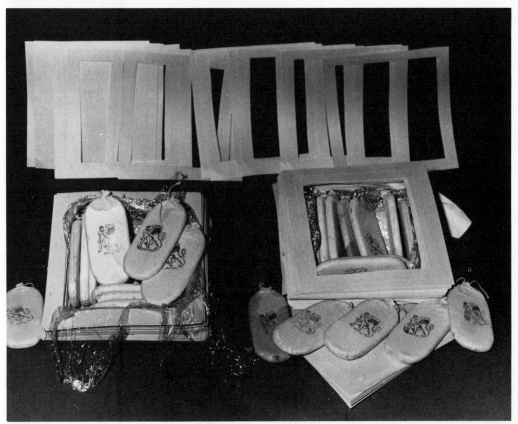

The increase in encounters with armed violators had been noted for some time, and the recent trend has been toward the use of deadly weapons against Customs officers. Two Customs Patrol officers were shot dead in April 1974 while on patrol along the U.S.–Mexican border at Nogales.

The traffickers, as they are called in the parlance of the seventies, have modernized their methods of operation with the use of aircraft, electronic devices such as radar, and couriers in bewildering disguises. The U.S. Customs Service, widely acknowledged as the world's most sophisticated and best-equipped enforcement and detection agency, always manages to keep ahead of its adversaries by utilizing long-range strategy, planning, counterintelligence. This running battle of wits is also a contest of willpower and determination, which must of necessity continue until human nature changes.

From diamonds to watch movements, from parrots to machine guns, from cocaine to heroin, from Irish whiskey to Japanese cameras—the list of taxable and prohibited items of merchandise on the "watch list" for Customs inspectors is endless and growing all the time. Motivated by greed, many individuals are willing to risk their lives and their freedom to "get by" Customs. But the vigilant Customs officers can be relied upon to do their duty, frequently in the face of great personal risk.

The Customs Service, rich in tradition, has always attracted men and women of outstanding achievement motivated by high idealism. It has included personalities famous in American history, men of letters, and many who achieved fame

On board ship, a Customs inspector discovers narcotics concealed in a wall behind the headboard of a bunk.

Narcotics concealed under a floor panel
near a ship hatchway.

and fortune in the world of trade and commerce. They brought to the service their experience and knowledge, to the advantage of the American people.

Too much praise cannot be given to the rank and file employee, the inspector, the agent, the appraiser, the attorney, the weigher, the measurer, the verifier, the aide, the secretary, all of whom carry on year after year in the service of their country. They carry out their duties, keenly conscious of the fact that they are part of one of the oldest federal agencies in the U.S. government, one which is closely linked to the economic future of the country.

Appendix

OFFICIALS WHO HAVE HEADED U.S. CUSTOMS SINCE 1871

Chiefs, Division of Customs	Dates	Appointed by Secretary of the Treasury
Henry B. James	1871–1875	George S. Boutwell
W. F. Clarke	1875–1879	Benjamin H. Bristow
Henry B. James	1879–1885	John Sherman
James G. Macgregor	1885–1893	Daniel Manning
John M. Comstock	1893–1899	John G. Carlisle
Andrew Johnson	1899–1903	Lyman J. Gage
John R. Garrison	1903–1905	L. M. Shaw
James L. Gerry	1905–1909	L. M. Shaw
Charles P. Montgomery	1909–1911	Franklin MacVeagh
Frank M. Halstead	1911–1919	Franklin MacVeagh
George W. Ashworth	1919–1922	Carter Glass

Commissioners of Customs

Ernest W. Camp Frank Dow, Acting Commissioner	4/16/27 to 5/15/29	Andrew W. Mellon
Francis X. A. Eble Frank Dow, Acting Commissioner	7/8/29 to 2/7/33	Andrew W. Mellon
James H. Moyle	7/18/33 to 9/6/39	William H. Woodin
Basil Harris Frank Dow, Acting Commissioner	9/7/39 to 7/15/40	Henry Morgenthau, Jr.
William R. Johnson Frank Dow, Acting Commissioner	7/19/40 to 6/17/47	Henry Morgenthau, Jr.
Frank Dow David B. Strubinger, Acting Commissioner	6/29/49 to 3/31/53	John W. Snyder
Ralph Kelly	3/29/54 to 1/20/61	George M. Humphrey
Philip Nichols, Jr.	3/24/61 to 9/30/64	Douglas Dillon
Lester D. Johnson	8/3/65 to 8/3/69	Henry H. Fowler
Myles J. Ambrose Edwin F. Rains, Acting Commissioner	8/5/69 to 2/5/72	David M. Kennedy
Vernon D. Acree	5/2/72 to present	John B. Connally*

* George P. Shultz replaced John B. Connally as the Secretary of the Treasury on June 12, 1972. William E. Simon replaced Mr. Shultz in 1974.

Index

Page numbers in italics indicate illustrations

169

fraud investigation, 12, 15–17. *See also* Fraud

inspecting and appraising imported merchandise, 6, *7*, 8, *8*, 12, 14

keeping data on availability of foreign oil, *111*, 112

putting stop to smuggling of stolen art objects, 129–33. *See also* Art Recovery Investigative Program

seizing smuggled merchandise, *9*, *13*, 14. *See also* Smuggling; Tactical interdiction units; Treasury Enforcement Communications System

war against narcotics, 6, 105, 107. *See also* Narcotics

international narcotics programs, 112–14

Cabinet Committee on International Narcotics Control (CCINC), 112–14

Customs Cooperation Council (CCC), 114

training programs for foreign Customs services, *112*, 113–14

Office of Enforcement Support, 108

Office of Investigations, 108–10

operational costs, 1960–73, *125*

personnel of. *See* Personnel of Customs Service

transfer of narcotics personnel and equipment to Drug Enforcement Administration of Justice Department, 108, 110

workload of, 1950–73, *125*

Customs Simplification Acts

archaic laws and practices revoked by, 90, 92

D

DABA (duty assessment by account), 115

Defense Department, 98

Detector dogs

use of, in war against narcotics, 133, *134*, 135–37

Dillon, Douglas, 95

Dow, Frank, 88, *88*, 89

"Drawback" procedure, 40, *41*

Drug(s). *See* Narcotics

Drug Abuse Law Enforcement (DALE), Office of, computer system of, 128

Drug Enforcement Administration of Justice Department, 107, 128

formation of, 108, 110

Duties

ad valorem, 52

defined, 52

liquidation of, 52, 90, 92

mixed, 52

new system of assessment, 114–15

"compliance by selectivity," 114–15

duty assessment by account (DABA), 115

specific, 52

E

Eble, Francis X. A., 81, *82*

Embargo Act of 1807, 56

and smuggling between the United States and Canada, 56–58, 60

Employees, Customs. *See* Personnel of Customs Service

Enforcement Support, Office of, 108

Espionage Act (1917), 73

F

Fish and Wildlife Service

import restrictions by, 98

Fitzsimmons, Thomas, 36

Food and Drug Administration

import restrictions by, 97

Foods

import restrictions on, 97

Foreign Assets Control Office

import restriction or prohibition by, 98

Fraud, to evade payment of import duties, 12, 15–17

"genteel" thievery, 17

investigation of, 12, 15

number of cases, 124

paid informants, 17

training personnel for, 16

penalties for, 12, 15, 17

G

Garfield, James A., 68

Grant, Ulysses S., 63, 67

H

Hamilton, Alexander, 35, 39, 46

Harris, Basil, 83